FREEDOM UNDERGROUND

Protesting the Iraq War in America

FREEDOM UNDERGROUND

Protesting the Iraq War in America

Carl Rising-Moore and Becky Oberg

Chamberlain Bros.
a member of Penguin Group (USA) Inc.
New York

Chamberlain Bros.
a member of
Penguin Group (USA) Inc.
375 Hudson Street
New York, NY 10014

An application has been submitted to register this book with the Library of Congress.

ISBN 1-59609-030-8

Printed in the United States of America

1 3 5 7 9 10 8 6 4 2

Book designed by Melissa Gerber.

Contents

Dedicated to Harriet Tubman (1820-1913), the African American woman who saved about three hundred slaves by helping them escape to the North and Canada.

Prologue

Death still is big business in Cuba, big business in the Balkans, big business in Afghanistan and Iraq. Death is big business, in fact, in more than one hundred countries on six different continents, and, when it comes in the form of American militarism, it is even expanding into outer space.

There are still those who dare to resist death in spite of the risks. There is a new Underground Railroad—the Freedom Underground—dedicated to sneaking military deserters out of the country. It targets those who would rather commit suicide than fight in Afghanistan, Iraq, or any other military target. To them, life as an expatriate, jail time, even death is preferable to serving in what they consider an unjust war. This is the story of some of those fugitives, their guides to freedom, and the journalist who observed it all.

Many people wonder why anyone would desert an all-volunteer military. Activist Sylvia Chambers addressed the issue in a speech before antiwar demonstrators. She said many "likely joined the military based on financial reasons and false hopes of benefits being cut daily by the Bush regime. Seeing signs 'Can you really afford to pass up $600 a month for college?' and realizing that could be their only chance to afford college." Many refer to this approach as the "poverty draft."

While there are some noble souls who enlist to serve their country, for many it's the way out of poverty and into school. When I enlisted in 2003, I had held a part-time dishwasher's job for two years, the only work I could find in spite of having earned a college degree. The Army offered me a full-time job and a chance to attend graduate school. Following my recruiter's advice, however, I "forgot" to mention I'd been treated for depression while in college. I enlisted for four years, then suffered a nervous breakdown during basic training and was medically discharged. (Although this problem is common, I wish to atone for it here and urge anyone considering doing this to apply for a waiver instead of enlisting under fraudulent circumstances and then confessing to it during the amnesty period).

Chambers also addressed stop-loss orders. "Many of the soldiers are being subjected to the 'stop-loss' orders, where even if their enlistment term was supposed to be over, they are forbidden to leave. According to *The Washington Post*, the Army alone has blocked the possible retirements and departures of more than 40,000 soldiers, about 16,000 of them National Guard and Reserve members who were eligible to leave the service this year." Some refer to this as a "backdoor draft."

Carl writes: "The only people of the world that do not know what the American government does around the world are Americans themselves. The mass media act more as embedded agents of the U.S. government than independent and freethinking journalists.

Americans, therefore, believe in most part what the media inform them to believe. A case in point is the *Indianapolis Star*, which ran two editorials offering their support to the Bush administration for an Iraq invasion. Some journalists have since apologized for accepting the lies of the Bush and Blair governments hook, line and sinker without questioning the validity of the information offered by their governments. Just as history had to be constantly rewritten to fit the facts in George Orwell's *1984*, so it is happening in Washington and London today."

In baseball, it's three strikes and you're out. George W. Bush, former co-owner of the Texas Rangers baseball team, a man interested in becoming the baseball commissioner before entering politics, should know the rules of the game. In justifying the invasion of Iraq, strike one was the revelation that there were no weapons of mass destruction, strike two the admission that there was no connection between Saddam Hussein and September 11, strike three to claim that this was a war of civilizations and that we had to defeat Saddam Hussein because he was a murdering, torturing tyrant. It's clear we have struck out. It's time to leave the game. It becomes clearer by the day that this war has nothing to do with civilizing and democratizing that part of the world. It is about geopolitics. It is about water. It's all about oil.

Chapter 1

Laying the Tracks

Fall 2003

All my Sisters and Brothers,

I have something that is heavy on my heart that I wish to share with you.

These e-mail lists are handy in that it gets the word out quickly. Please pass it on to other lists.

The deaths of our troops in Iraq was inevitable, as well as the even greater collateral damage (dead infants and noncombatants). My wife Lisa was the only person that I shared the feeling I had that this war would not be over quickly and that it would turn out like Afghanistan did for the Russians. My hope was that I was wrong in my assessment before we waged war on Iraq. Now, we have people coming from all over the Muslim world to kill our troops for God. The idea that America has launched a crusade upon the Muslim world by extremist Christians will be hard to dispel. If we admit that it was about positioning America within a geopolitical advantage for oil and world dominance, it would not help matters any. The truth is the truth. Senator Bayh last night made his [prowar] comments on the Senate floor. Senator Lugar's staff told me that he plans to approve the $87 billion. Since, he talks about another $50 billion for rebuilding Iraq. They should all be brought to the World Court and charged with war crimes and crimes against humanity. They (all those in Congress and the Senate) that voted for this war should also be charged. Their punishment should be to live in the same conditions that we have placed the prisoners in Cuba.

Now I hear about our troops killing themselves to avoid further duty in Iraq. Perhaps some of these deaths are a result of personal relationships back home falling apart. As they said in the U.S. Army, Jody has your girl and gone. Whatever.

This is my plan of action. Words are fine, but in the bottom line I believe that Action Speaks Louder Than Words.

I will be going back to the country of my birth soon. There, I will speak to people from across Canada to receive our troops that no longer wish to remain in the military. I have not spoken to any lawyers about my plan, but when I hear about these women and men that would kill themselves to escape, my duty as a veteran and a loyal American is to fight my government in whatever nonviolent manner is appropriate. I know that when I push the send button, these words will be in the hands of Ashcroft and friends soon. If I am arrested as a result, please would someone take this message to my Sisters and Brothers in Canada that would receive these troops?

Now is the time to act. If we do not, W. will be in the White House for another 4 years.

Stand up and be counted, my friends and activists. This country is worth fighting for, and it is better than what we have become. I will keep you posted on the Freedom Underground if possible.

Your Brother in Peace and Justice,

Carl

P.S. If you know of anyone that wishes to escape to

Canada, have them call me. Please tell them not to speak about their desire, only that they would like to meet with me face to face. If they live anywhere in the Midwest, they can come here. If they live outside of the Midwest have them give me a nickname and a telephone number at a phone booth or a nonmilitary friend's home. I will contact them on a secure phone, as the number above is not secure nor is this message.

[Any nation that did not join the Coalition of the Willing could be a safe possibility for asylum.]

Václav Havel once said dissidents were thrown into their roles. "You do not become a 'dissident' just because you decide one day to take up this most unusual career," he said. "You are thrown into it by your personal sense of responsibility, combined with a complex set of external circumstances. You are cast out of the existing structures and placed in a position of conflict with them. It begins as an attempt to do your work well, and ends with being branded an enemy of society." He was right—that's exactly what happened with me.

I (Becky) am a freelance reporter. At an anti-Bush

rally, I signed up for an e-mail list for peace activists, figuring it would be a good way to get tips on potential stories. I expected to be covering speeches and rallies. I did not expect to witness federal felonies and military crimes. Nor did I expect my story to encourage people to commit federal felonies and military crimes.

As Havel said, I was thrown into it. I believed, and still believe, that the public has a right to know things are so bad that some people are willing to risk everything and desert their post in the Armed Forces. I picked up my notebook, called Carl Rising-Moore and requested an interview. After the interview, I did some research and learned two lessons.

First, deserting soldiers aren't aggressively chased at this time. A federal arrest warrant is issued, meaning that any local, state or federal law enforcement officer can apprehend the deserter. One recent example—a deserter was spotted breaking into his own house one night—he was locked out. The cops questioned him and found the outstanding warrant. There is no statute of limitations for desertion—it's 2004 and deserters from the Vietnam War could still be arrested if caught in the

United States (President Jimmy Carter's amnesty policy covered only draft resisters—those who peacefully evaded the draft by traveling abroad or failing to register. Military deserters were not covered in the pardon).

Second, it is extremely difficult to gain a conscientious objector (CO) discharge. During the Gulf War (Desert Storm), the military granted III CO discharges before stopping the practice, resulting in 2,500 service members going to jail, according to the Center on Conscience and War (CCW). Some COs were shipped to Kuwait, told they could not apply for CO status, or told they could apply only after they'd gone to war.

During the Iraq War, two conscientious objectors— one in the Army and one in the Marine Corps—had two very different fates during Operation Iraqi Freedom. A Marine reservist, Lance Corporal Steven Funk, went to prison for his beliefs. Army Private First Class Jeremy Hinzman fled to Canada with his wife and son.

Funk publicly declared himself a conscientious objector. He was on Unauthorized Absence (UA, the

Marine version of absent without leave—AWOL) when he reported back to his base in San Jose, California, on April 1. Funk was acquitted of desertion but convicted of UA. He was sentenced to six months in the Camp Lejeune brig, forfeiture of two-thirds pay for six months, reduction to the rank of private and a bad-conduct discharge. He became a symbol of resistance in the United States and around the world.

Hinzman, a Catholic who was influenced by Buddhism and attended Quaker services, applied for conscientious objector status. He was sent to Afghanistan when his son Liam was seven months old. He washed dishes in a non-combatant role, and worked grueling twelve- to sixteen-hour shifts seven days a week, allegedly to serve as an example. When he returned to the United States, Liam was walking and did not recognize him. Hinzman believes his conscientious objector status was denied because he admitted he would fight in self-defense. When he learned his unit would be sent to Iraq for an "indefinite deployment," he knew he would either serve in Iraq, refuse and be court-martialed, or flee to another country. He did not want to lose any more time with Liam, so he fled to Canada and sought political asylum. He was compared to the many draftavoiders and deserters who sought refuge in Canada during the Vietnam War.

Two young men, two very different stories. When I first interviewed Carl, Funk was in the brig and Hinzman had not yet deserted. The last execution for desertion was also the only firing squad execution since the Civil War: Army Private Eddie Slovik, executed for desertion in northwestern Europe during World War II. According to historian Steven Ambrose, "They felt an example had to be made."

An example lost on Carl.

"I'm not afraid of Ashcroft or George Bush," he said. He mentioned the gaps in Bush's military record. I learned Carl was an Army veteran, and that he had been sympathetic to draft resisters and deserters during the Vietnam War. He'd volunteered for combat duty in Vietnam but was kept stateside, which he later was grateful for. He'd become a nonviolent activist, dedicated to opposing the government when it acted unjustly. "We have a fascist regime, and we have to fight it through nonviolent means," he said. "I would hope the American people would stand up against this fascist regime of George W. Bush, the unelected military dictator of the United States of America."

Would the Army still pursue execution? "Obviously it's an option," said one spokesperson. "I don't think so. The last time was World War II," said another.

I had both sides. I ran the article in the November 5-12, 2003, issue of *Nuvo*, an alternative weekly in Indianapolis, Indiana.

I didn't expect the number of responses I received. One was from the United Kingdom. Two people volunteered to help with the Freedom Underground. Others voiced their support for the AWOL service members and their opposition to the war. Carl and a woman in the network both posted in the comments section on *Nuvo*'s web page.

Carl wrote:

Sisters and Brothers,

There is much interest in helping those that are in the

military presently.

Very few believed that they would be placed in combat in an illegal and immoral war.

The majority of military personnel in Iraq now believe they are sitting ducks. The morale sinks with every passing day.

After the rocket attack on the Black Hawk helicopter that killed another six military personnel several days ago, other soldiers went on a shooting spree that used rocket fire and heavy caliber shells against "suspected hideouts" of the enemy. There was no mention of how many were killed in these attacks, but it is exactly what happened in 'Nam when surviving soldiers would kill anything that moved in retaliation to their friend's death. And so it goes. It is hard not to engage in a mob mentality when your fellow troops are killed. But yet, that is the task at hand. To preserve your humanity while being attacked by the "enemy."

Every soldier that survived Nam that I know has problems coping with what happened there. If you become a cold-blooded killer in Iraq, you will bring that back home. Keep your head down and apply for noncombat status. You will be the real heroes. May you survive this ordeal and return to your loved ones soon.

If enough troops quit fighting, the war will end that much sooner. Save your lives and your humanity because it is not worth killing or being killed for. Chickenhawk [George W. Bush] has nothing but a mouth, "bring 'em on." He lied about the justification for war and our troops die daily. When will it end?

To eliminate those in opposition to the U.S. and British occupation of Iraq, it would require carpet bombing with nuclear bombs from one end of Iraq to the other. That will not happen, because that would make the problem of stealing Iraq's oil impossible.

If anyone wishes to escape this double-talking administration while in the military, I will have some contacts soon to report. If you are going to leave the country, do not wait until you are AWOL. Make your move while still on leave.

Do not travel in uniform and wear a baseball cap if your hair is military style. My friends north of the border are good people and interested in doing whatever is required of them.

The Pentagon has decided to send more troops to Germany and Europe for R & R instead of returning them to the continental U.S. Norway, Sweden and Finland have a long history of protecting our soldiers that have had enough of this mess. Again, do not wait until your leave is finished before leaving if that is your choice.

If you require counseling, my cell number is (xxx) xxx-xxxx.

Do not call me from your home phone number or a government phone because this cell number is not secure. Do not give me your correct name or service, it is not necessary. If you choose to leave the country, remember that it may be years before you can return. It was during the Carter administration that amnesty was given to those that fled the USA to avoid the Vietnam War draft. This decision is a serious undertaking, and should not be decided without counseling. But as I stated in the article by Becky Oberg, "If everything else fails, people should desert, just as George W. Bush did during the Vietnam War."

Carl Rising-Moore

A woman in the network wrote:

There are so many men who signed their name at that post office on their eighteenth birthday but have no idea what to do now.

Our Web site will help. There are many alternatives and yes, the wind of the draft will soon be a hurricane.

AFSC [American Friends Service Committee] has excellent resources as well.

If you need money to buy that book or just want to look for alternative direction, please visit our site.

> . . .Just a Taoist hermit
> on the side of a mountain
> who listens for that train
> whistle whenever it's near. . .

The story went beyond Indianapolis. Several antiwar Web sites picked it up. Antiwar activists in Canada reran it. The article was even translated into Italian, Spanish, Greek and Polish. While publicity was risky to the network—the federal government and the military now knew it existed— publicity was also beneficial. Other activists pledged their support, be it financial, moral or physical.

The tracks were laid. Soon the passengers would arrive.

Chapter 2

All Aboard

2/29/2004

0438

To: Carl Rising-Moore

From: Brandon Hughey

Please help a desperate serviceman

Carl Rising-Moore,

I am a member of the U.S. military whose unit deploys to Iraq next week. I do not want to be a pawn in the government's war for oil, and have told my superiors that I want out of the military. They are not willing to chapter me out and tell me that I have no choice but to pack my bags and get ready to go to Iraq. This has led me to feel hopeless and I have thought about suicide several times. However, just a few days ago I discovered some articles about you and Freedom Underground on the Internet, which gave me new hope. I am desperate enough that I would gladly leave the country if that's what it meant to escape. I do not have much money, however, and would need a place to stay and help finding a job once I left the country. I pray that you or someone you know can help me. I am in Texas, I won't tell you exactly where because I don't know who could be reading this but I am willing to pack my bags and start driving to anywhere you tell me to go. I pray that you get this letter as my unit deploys next week and I don't have much time. Please write back as soon as you can. God bless you and what you are doing.

Brandon

Indianapolis

3/2/2004

0928

We're waiting for a fleeing service member outside a Safeway grocery store. He'll be a passenger on the Freedom Underground, an underground network dedicated to sneaking deserters out of the country.

According to Carl Rising-Moore, the conductor of this new underground railroad, he's not the first. Nor will he be the last—Rising-Moore told me that several Muslim service members, along with many others, have considered deserting rather than fighting in Iraq. While he encourages people to use the legal channels to leave the military and others in the network encourage desertion only as a last resort, Rising-Moore counsels suicidal service members to leave immediately. This passenger, Army Private Brandon David Hughey, is stationed at Ft. Hood, Texas. He found my article about the Freedom Underground on the antiwar site www.duckdaotsu.org, a Web page run by a Taoist hermit in the Rocky Mountains.

Another irony—Indianapolis is home of the U.S. Army Deserter Information Point (USADIP). Brandon's right under their noses, so close that he can't afford any mistakes. Carl told him to turn off his cell phone so he's harder to track. He'll have to hide his vehicle. He'll also have to get rid of his military ID and dog tags.

Carl answered Brandon's plea for help because he

was on the brink of suicide. One night he sat on his bunk with a bottle of pills in his hand, ready to take them rather than report for duty in Iraq. Something stopped him and led him to Carl. While Carl prefers people "mess with the system from within" and use legal means to oppose the war, he recommends suicidal service members leave immediately.

Indianapolis

3/2/2004

1420

I followed Carl and Brandon to a safe house in downtown Indianapolis. Brandon hid his dog tags and military ID in the trunk of his gray Mustang, which he and Carl then hid in the safe house's junk-laden garage. Brandon is wearing a New York Knicks baseball cap to hide his "high and tight," or military haircut. He has only his driver's license and high school diploma to identify himself—will that be enough? Canada usually requires Americans to present a photo identification and proof of citizenship, such as a birth certificate. A passport meets both requirements, but Brandon does not have one.

He's been in the Army since July 2003, and known he could be deployed since December of the same year. He got his deployment orders a few days ago—his unit is leaving for the Middle East as he arrives at the safe house.

His story is familiar. "Growing up, I always thought it was a good thing to do, go into the military," he told the Canadian Broadcasting Corporation (CBC) at the end of our journey. "After high school, I figured it'd be a good way to get money to go to college." He's seen soldiers in his company suffer nervous breakdowns due to the fighting in Iraq.

He's survived this long—why is he running now? He feels that suicide or desertion are his only options, due to it being mere days before his unit deploys. Some will consider him a hero—he's risking jail time rather than supporting a war he believes is unjust. Some will consider him a coward and a traitor—he is deserting in a time of war. There is no easy choice for this desperate young man from San Angelo, Texas.

He enlisted for four years when he was seventeen. His father had to sign a form giving him permission to enlist, as Brandon was not yet a legal adult. Carl shakes his head. "He's not old enough to sign for himself, but he's old enough to die?"

Brandon did not tell anyone he was considering suicide. He's seen how the military humiliates suicidal soldiers—a guard with the soldier 24/7, a sergeant or officer screaming insults about the soldier's mental stability, confiscation of weapons and shoelaces. A staff sergeant said that officers take the shoelaces to isolate the soldier, not to protect them.

Carl knows that aiding this eighteen-year-old man is illegal, but he doesn't think it's wrong. He believes the war is unjust and civil disobedience is mandatory. Compliance "goes against the Nuremberg principle," he explains. According to the Nuremberg principle, a person has the obligation to disobey laws his or her conscience dictates are unjust. By not engaging in civil disobedience when one's conscience urges it, he says, one breaks international law. "You're breaking international law by not breaking domestic law," Carl says. "The United States broke international law by following the Bush Doctrine of preemptive war. Every soldier has a responsibility to stop fighting."

By running?

"This is the place to fight America," Carl says. "America needs fighting by speaking the truth. . . . America is the most appropriate place to fight the Bush Doctrine. Truth is the weapon against this current administration that went to war based on lies. It's the only weapon we've got."

Indianapolis
3/3/2004
Nighttime

I'm at the safe house in downtown Indianapolis, armed with a camera, notebook, pen and a video camera. I will be writing this story for *Nuvo* and filming it for the Canadian Broadcasting Corporation (CBC). I will ride along with Carl as he escorts Brandon across the border. Carl encourages Brandon to use civilian duffel bags instead of the military bag he brought along.

"Do you have anything else that's military?" he asks.

"I have an M16 magazine," he replies. Carl and I wince. He holds up the magazine. "It's not loaded," he says. It's little relief to either of us.

"We've got to get rid of it," says Carl. The trip will commence as soon as we find a safe and unincriminating way to dispose of the magazine.

Getting rid of an M16 magazine in Indianapolis at night is not an easy task. We drove around the city, trying to think of something. We couldn't sell it on the black market. None of the sporting goods stores had a bullet buyback program. Even if one did, it's not like an M16 is used for hunting. We couldn't just casually throw it away; it had to be taken to the landfill quickly and have little potential of being found before then. We were in a bad neighborhood when Carl pulled into a gas station. Suddenly, he had an idea.

He dug through one of the trash cans, and then carefully placed the magazine inside. He covered it with more trash. Not exactly the safest way to dispose of the magazine, but it would work. If someone found it, it might not seem too out of place in a bad neighborhood. The trash would be taken away the next day, so it was quick. Now the trip could begin.

Somewhere in Ohio
3/3/2004
2320

This fog is straight out of a bad mystery novel. It forces Carl to slow down at times. Then it'll suddenly dissipate, and we'll continue down the interstate at an average of 65 m.p.h. We're somewhere in northern Ohio. The original plan was to enter Canada through the Detroit-Windsor border, but that's changed. Now the plan is to go to Buffalo and cross at Niagara Falls.

I look for the North Star, but the fog has obscured it. Somehow it seems fitting. The fog of deception has obscured the vision of the American people. The fog of accusations of treason and being unpatriotic has obscured moral courage shown in dissent. The blinding fog does not change the fact that the North Star is shining, and the metaphorical fog does not change the truth.

Brandon, a tank driver, doesn't dare to drive the vehicle—we've borrowed it from a woman who doesn't know what we're doing. It's a nondescript vehicle, with an American flag decal on the back windshield and a "Pacers Fan" plate on the front of it. If pulled over, Brandon would have to present ID—the last thing he wants to do, for obvious reasons. He's listening to music in the backseat. He seems calm, everything considered.

The three of us have talked about our various experiences in the Army. When the discussion shifts to politics, opinions of Bush or views on the war, I stay silent; I'm just along to document the story, but it's hard to remain impartial. Part of me wants to say "Snap out of it, soldier!" and encourage him to return to his unit; part of me is sympathetic to his situation.

Carl explains the Bush Doctrine in neighborhood terms. For example, say neighbor A tells you that neighbor B has a small-scale armory in the house. That neighbor B has weapons of mass destruction. Do you need to appeal to the authorities, or do you have the right to go in and attack neighbor B? According to the Bush Doctrine, you have the right to break into neighbor B's house and attack neighbor B.

Brandon laughs at the analogy. "Even if it's not his intent to use them?"

"Or even if he doesn't have any," says Rising-Moore.

Brandon is from a Republican family and originally supported the war. Then he began doing research into what he was fighting for. He learned about international law and how it specifically forbids the invasion of a sovereign nation and preemptive war. His commanders told him that thinking was not his job. As he learned there was no sign of the weapons of mass destruction, that the "mobile weapons labs" turned out to be weather stations, that much of the intelligence was falsified or faulty, he realized the pretext of the war wasn't what he'd been told. He decided the war was illegal under international law, his contract was null and void, and anything was better than supporting the war.

As we head towards the Canadian border,

Brandon's unit has arrived in Kuwait.

He's been gone for more than twenty-four hours, so he's officially absent without leave. His unit has been deployed, so he has missed movement by design, another military offense. The maximum punishment for missing movement by design is a dishonorable discharge, forfeiture of all pay and allowances and confinement for two years. Ten days after his disappearance, his family will receive a letter asking them to urge him to return to military control. In thirty days, he'll be dropped from his unit's rolls and administratively classified as a deserter. Desertion during a time of war is a capital offense, a fact we all know but don't discuss. Surely Bush would decide the political risks were too great. Surely he wouldn't order the execution of a deserter. . . . or would he?

Eddie Slovik was the last soldier executed for desertion. According to reports, 3,800 soldiers deserted in 2002 and 3,255 were returned to military control, a recapture rate of about 85 percent. In 2001, 5,065 deserted and 4,966 were returned, a recapture rate of about 98 percent.

Somewhere in Pennsylvania

3/5/2004

1006

We spent the night in a Motel 6 outside of Cleveland. In the morning, the men pulled out a U.S. map and tried to navigate the best route to Canada. I snapped a few pictures on my regular camera and updated my notes. It was almost time to move out.

I filmed Carl and Brandon leaving the motel room and going to the car. I also filmed our route with a video camera, using my finger to show where on the map each location was.

Our destination is St. Catherine's, a small Ontario town just a few miles from the longest unmilitarized border in the world. Crossing the border will be the riskiest part of our journey—if the Army has already issued a warrant for Brandon's arrest, he could be caught at the border. If he is caught, all three of us could go to jail. Brandon is nervous, and Carl teaches him some deep breathing exercises. We are all worried about what could happen.

Brandon tells us the military has tried to keep returning personnel separate from deploying personnel. It's easy to understand why when he talks about what he's heard. "You have to worry more about the sand flies than the suicide bombers," he says. He's heard service members in Iraq are getting incurable skin diseases from the sand flies. Both sides are suffering from the use of depleted uranium, the effects of which will last long after the war is over. There are rumors some soldiers have died from dehydration due to a tight water ration. Some of the Humvees aren't properly armored, including the ones he was supposed to drive.

It isn't clear how much of that is true, but there are reports that morale is abysmal. The suicide rate is higher than normal; the Pentagon sent a team of experts over to Iraq to address the problem. Some soldiers were not given a proper pre-deployment physical, which resulted in medical evacuations for everything from mental health reasons to asthma to heart conditions. There is no exit strategy. Most damning; no sign of the weapons of mass destruction.

Brandon, a Catholic, believes his orders are contrary to international law. "I thought what was going on over there was immoral," he told the CBC later. "It wasn't right. . . I feel that since Bush broke that international law, that every soldier has the responsibility to resist it." He's not alone in his assessment. Some coalition troops are refusing to fight—British, Turkish, American. . . .One American soldier and Afghanistan veteran, Jeremy Hinzman, has applied for political asylum in Canada. Others looking to desert have contacted Hinzman for help, but Carl considers that to be his job.

We're close to the border now. The plan is to cross during rush hour so the Canadian guards won't grill us as intensely. There's time to kill and we're exhausted. We drive past a motel with a sign advertising $20 rooms. Perfect.

The clerk explains the $20 rate is only for a few hours. We assure him that is all we want. He seems nervous about renting to us. I know what he's thinking:

A man in his fifties, a teenage male and a woman in her twenties. They probably want to do something illegal. When Carl asks for an extra bed, the clerk informs us that'll be another $15. Fine. We check in and walk to the room.

I collapse onto one bed, Carl lies down on the other bed and Brandon takes the couch. Within minutes, we're all sound asleep. The motel has a strange scent and is obviously a "no questions asked" place, but it meets the criteria. It's cheap and we can sleep there. We wake up refreshed—we'll seem more alert when we cross the border.

A woman laughs at us when we ask when rush hour is; the border's rarely that busy. We'll aim for around 4:30. We still have time, so we decide to go for a walk around Niagara.

There's a small park near the river. American and Canadian flags flank a small replica of the Statue of Liberty. What a backdrop! I pull out the camera and start filming. "What does liberty mean to you?"

Brandon starts to answer. Freedom. Not having to fight in a war he doesn't believe in. The freedom to say no.

It's time. Carl prepares a contingency plan and advises Brandon on what to do if arrested. He tells Brandon he's been arrested before for acts of civil disobedience, and not to be afraid. Brandon starts doing the deep breathing Carl taught him. I turn off the video camera, and we climb back into the car. We drive onto Rainbow Bridge.

'The CBC is waiting for us. At their request, we've agreed to stay in the leftmost lane. Their camera crew is filming us cross. We slowly creep toward the border. The cover story should hold up: We're visiting colleges in New York and we decided to cross into Canada to watch the Knicks-Raptors game. A guard is walking along the bridge, checking for anything or anyone suspicious. He starts to walk over to our car, but suddenly turns around and goes back to talk to the CBC camera crew.

We pull up to the Canadian guard station and surrender our IDs. How do we know each other? Brandon may some day be Carl's son-in-law—won't his daughter be surprised?—and I'm a friend. Where are we going in Canada? We're going to watch the game, see our Knicks hats? The Raptors are playing the Pacers next week; we want to know how the Raptors play. How long will we be in Canada? Not long. Carl does the talking. The guard examines our IDs, then hands them back to us and lets us through. We're quiet until we get about fifty feet into Canada.

Brandon sighs in relief. "Safe from Bush's henchmen for the time being," he says.

"For a long time to come," Carl replies.

Brandon nods. "I feel safe now," he says. "I'm glad to be in this country. . . .I feel like a free man."

We meet up with the CBC and drive into St. Catherine's, Ontario. A group of the Society of Friends—Quakers—is waiting for us. "Welcome to Canada!" says Don Alexander, smiling. He chuckles, and says, "Or should that be, 'Welcome to Canada, eh?'" We all laugh, feeling more relaxed now that we have arrived. They invite us inside and offer us food, then offer to let us spend the night.

Quakers have a philosophy of never turning away anyone in need. They also have a fierce commitment to nonviolence. It's easy to understand why they would help. "Why would we say no?" says Rose Marie Cipryk, when asked why they're helping. "How could we? How could we not help him?"

Many of the Quakers are veterans of the underground; several of them helped deserters during the Vietnam War. Many believe history is repeating itself. They praise Brandon for his courage, and then turn to me to make sure I understand why they consider him a hero. They believe it takes great moral courage to refuse on conscience to fight a war. We set up a TV and watch the Knicks win, but we're more focused on our conversation than the game.

"He shouldn't have to go die in some killing fields in Iraq—or anywhere else—in a preemptive war that's totally contrary to international law," Carl says. The Friends nod in agreement. "He's a nice young man and he deserves a life."

The CBC has to finish their story, and take Brandon and Carl downstairs for more interviews. They ask us to be quiet and not walk around; the microphones will pick up that background noise. After a moment, one of the

Quakers says, "Let's go to worship." We close our eyes and listen for the voice of God.

They remember feeling great danger around the time we were crossing the border and had gone into worship. Had we been turned back, Brandon could have been arrested. One Quaker says she does not believe in a personal God, but, if she did, she would say He helped us across the border. They reflect on their history of nonviolence, regardless of the personal cost. I think about my risk in printing the story. I hope God will give me the strength to stand firm and to run the piece.

Maybe we all have moments where our moral courage is tested. Maybe mine is just beginning. The public has a right to know things are so bad over in Iraq that service members are risking jail time or life in exile—possibly even death—to avoid the war. Telling the story, however, is risky. What is truth worth?

St. Catherine's, Ontario
3/6/2004
Morning

We spend the night with the Friends, the first real sleep any of us have had on the trip. They present Brandon with an original, postcard-sized painting titled *The Angel of Grace*. He seems sad to see Carl go, but Carl tries to encourage him. "You're a different kind of soldier now," he says, calling him a soldier for peace. He helps him contact another deserter, Jeremy Hinzman, and a lawyer, Jeffry House, to help him gain legal status in Canada.

Brandon says leaving his family behind is the hardest part about deserting. I ask about his unit. "I hope they all make it back okay," he says. "It's just too bad they have to be over there in an illegal war." Any advice for service members in his situation? "If you're at that point, you're ready to take your own life, pack your bags and go."

He didn't know applying for conscientious objector status was an option. That status is difficult to get. According to the Center on Conscience and War, an organization that advises soldiers of their rights and how to get CO status (and, incidentally, does not recommend or encourage desertion as it is breaking the law), only a small percentage of people who apply receive a CO discharge. The applications take an average of six months to one year to process, sometimes as long as two years. The United States military does not recognize conditional conscientious objectors—for example, someone who would fight in what he or she considers a "just war" but refuse to fight in an "unjust war".

During the Gulf War, the Army granted CO status to III soldiers before putting a stop to the practice, according to CCW. As a result, 2,500 soldiers were sent to prison for refusing to fight. According to the CCW's Bill Gavlin, during that war a number of COs in Camp Lejeune were "beaten, harassed and treated horribly." While Gavlin does not know of any incidents like that in this war, he has counseled service members who were harassed. One woman was threatened with court-martial if she applied. It is not an offense to apply, and Gavlin says her superiors did it "to intimidate her." According to *The New York Times*, the Army granted five conscientious objector discharges in

January of 2004. The Army granted thirty-one conscientious objector discharges in 2003, seventeen in 2002, and a mere nine in 2001.

When we cross the border, a Marine recruiting billboard greets Carl and me. "Look at that garbage," he says, disgusted. " 'The change is forever.' Yeah, if you're dead, that's pretty much forever."

He tells me about a conversation he had with his wife before we left. "I'm scared," he told her. "I've got to do what I've got to do. I don't want to do this. I have to."

When we return to America, he establishes the Dove Legal Defense Fund to help cover the legal expenses of current and future Freedom Underground passengers.

3/28/2004
9:19 p.m.
To: Carl Rising-Moore
From: Brandon Hughey

Dear Carl,
Glad to hear that my dad picked up my car. My lawyer

Jeff will be trying to get ahold of him to discuss the claim that the Army will discharge me. We want to be a little suspicious of this however as it may be a trick to get me back on U.S. soil. If they are willing to help me, however, it would make things much easier and it would definitely be a big victory showing that even the Army will back down if one has the courage to stand up to them. I will probably send an e-mail to my dad sometime soon and hopefully Jeff will be able to establish contact with him as well. Thank you for all your help and all that you have done.

Sincerely,

Brandon

5/18/2004

4:01 a.m.

To: Carl Rising-Moore

From: Brandon Hughey

Dear Carl,

I received this e-mail message just now. It is short and abbreviated because it was sent from a cell phone.

(HELP deplying soon)on cellph. moblize 2 fthood

*tmrw! need info to goto canada. plz respnd w/ph # or info.
I lk 4wrd to join u&jeremy*

His e-mail address is: *x@.x.x* I gave him your e-mail
address but told him I would forward this to you to help speed
things up. Perhaps you can give him a phone number at which
to contact you. I hope that you can help him. As soon as I am
back on my feet financially I will do everything I can to assist this
noble cause. I am starting to get more and more support from
Canadian Labor unions such as Cuppe and the CAW. Perhaps
the next time I speak to these unions I will ask for help in assisting
the growing numbers of soldiers who write to me seeking help in
getting to Canada. I think I've heard from four or five soldiers
so far seeking such assistance. I passed along your e-mail
address. Have you heard from any of them? Thank you again
for such brave and unselfish work.

Sincerely,

Brandon

5/20/2004

2:32 a.m.

To: Carl Rising-Moore

From: Brandon Hughey

Carl,

I will let our friend know about reading between the lines. Did you discuss anything with him? When I talk with him, I will try and find out more about his situation. I will pass on the advice you sent to me. The situation in Iraq just gets worse. The Associated Press just released an article 37 minutes ago about U.S. gunships attacking a "suspected safe house of foreign fighters" and killing 40-45 innocent civilians. You may have heard about the incident by now. They were supposedly having a wedding celebration and fired celebratory gunfire into the air. U.S. helicopters then closed in on the place and shot it up. The saddest part is about 10-15 of the casualties were children. . . I am so thankful that I am not taking part in this mess.

Brandon

5/28/2004
2:51 a.m.
To: Becky Oberg
From: Brandon Hughey

Becky,

Sorry it's taken a while to respond. I've been quite busy. . .

First of all, the Iraq war was launched without the backing of the U.N. Security Council, which is against U.N. law on preemptive war. It was declared a violation of the U.N. Charter by Kofi Annan and Hans Blix. In short, it is illegal.

Second of all, the pretenses under which George Bush launched the war were so blatantly false. The main reasons he gave for attacking Iraq were to find Saddam Hussein's weapons of mass destruction, and that he was connected to terrorism. As the war dragged on, no such weapons were found. Not only that, but President Bush has since admitted that Saddam Hussein had no ties to terrorist organizations. While it is true that Saddam was a cruel dictator, people do not like liberators who flatten their cities with bombs and carelessly kill large numbers of the civilian population.

The prison abuse scandal does not surprise me. In the Army, you are trained to believe that your enemy is less than human. This is because it makes it easier to kill them.. The Army doesn't teach its soldiers directly to torture and humiliate people, but soldiers who are sent to Iraq have been trained that their enemies are subhuman, so obviously they are going to treat them as such. People have been so shocked over this, and rightfully so, but this is the mind-set that the Army drills into its troops during their training.

The attitude in Canada overall has been quite supportive. Polls have shown that 75 percent of Canadians are against the war in Iraq, so I suppose it makes sense that they would be supportive of a soldier who does not want to fight this war for the same reasons that they themselves did not support it.

It's hard to say at this point how I would be able to help the network. However, through the experiences that I have had, I believe that I would be able to give advice to soldiers who are in the same situation I was in. I would also like to use the attention that my case has been getting to build more support in Canada for U.S. war resisters, and hopefully make it a little bit easier for people who decide to follow in my footsteps.

The State Department is not trying to extradite me. There is legally nothing they can do to have me extradited, because for that to take place, a refugee claimant must have committed a crime in both the U.S. and Canada. Deserting the U.S. Army is not a crime in Canada, so my claim will receive the same legal process that any other refugee claim would. Also, I was told by a reporter from The San Antonio Express News who called the State Department for a story he was working on that an Army spokesperson has said that they would not pursue me.

Brandon

"Individuals have international duties which transcend the national obligations of obedience. . . Therefore [individual citizens] have the duty to violate domestic laws to prevent crimes against peace and humanity from occurring."

—*Nuremberg War Crimes Tribunal*

Chapter 3

The Stationmasters

Each deserter has a different path. Brandon wasn't the only one who went to Canada—I know that deserters went to different places throughout the country. At least one went to the Netherlands, although that country supported the Iraq War. There are two main criteria for a destination: the government of the country did not support the Iraq War, the country would be likely to accept a deserter—Canadians prefer the term "war resister"—and not extradite him or her back to the U.S. At the time Canada's government was interested in "repairing" relations with the United States (although Canada still did not support the war in Iraq), but an election was coming up. A good chunk of Canadian immigration law involved delay, which would work to the war resisters' favor. A good deal of politics would factor in as well.

There were a growing number of safe houses on this network, which may not have been the only network to help fleeing service members. A woman in the Rocky Mountains ran one of them. She agreed to an interview on the condition I did not use her real name. I named the woman Mara Veritas—mara meaning "bitter" in Hebrew and veritas meaning "truth" in Latin. She was a Taoist hermit on the side of a mountain, although she had Internet access and a cell phone. Bitter truth: it seemed to fit.

Mara refers to herself as the "caboose of the train." She grew up in South Dakota, where she had many Lakota friends. Many of them were drafted for the Vietnam War, and many of them died. All of the race and class distinctions in the draft bothered her. A VISTA worker in Hot Springs told her about the draft and the need for safe places. She was motivated to be one of those safe places, and helped her first war resister sneak across the border when she was fourteen.

"That's how I got started," she said.

She moved to Denver after her ex-brother-in-law beat her for having an American flag on the floor. She became an activist there, read Gandhi and Tolstoy, and housed deserters.

"We got [the war] in our living rooms," she said, reflecting on the differences between coverage during Vietnam and coverage of this war. "The war was in our living rooms and we knew it."

One day (back during Vietnam) a man in "big, black, shiny FBI shoes" was photographing her house. Undaunted, she grabbed her camera and started photographing the agent, who quickly retreated. Later, when they asked her about a deserter she was housing, she quickly notified him to flee to Canada. She later ran into the agent when they were attending 12-step meetings.

She regrets how Vietnam veterans were treated. Her theory why they were treated so roughly is tied to the drug culture. She said it was hard to be around high vets as they would start telling horrific stories

CARL RISING-MOORE AND BECKY OBERG

about what they did in the war. Mara strongly suspects they suffered from post-traumatic stress disorder, but it was not a recognized mental illness back then.

She has once again opened her home to deserters. "We're a safe house here," Mara said. She has a car that gets good gas mileage in her driveway—it's reserved specifically for deserters. "If that's the car they need to get to Canada, then that's the car they'll take to Canada," Mara said.

"I have no choice," Mara said. "I am a person of conscience. . . . It is my duty and I cannot live with myself if I don't."

She referred to soldiers as "slaves of the state whose civil liberties are stripped away." That said, "I would not recommend [desertion]." She said it should be the "very, very, very, very last resort." However, she will help a person in that situation.

"If I see something wrong, I will take a stand," she said. "It will not be a violent stand, but it will be a stand. . . . Yes, we can make a difference. Individuals can make a difference."

Mara also runs an "anti-war, pro-GI" Web site,

www.duckdaotsu.org. The site features a tribute to slain soldiers and "people who fought the fight and thought they were doing the right thing." The site also features coverage of the rumored draft, which currently has bills in both houses of Congress (the Senate version is S89, the House versions is HR 163). It also has information on Freedom Underground, registering as a conscientious objector, news of the war and Taoist meditations. This is the web site Brandon Hughey visited before he deserted.

Jesus never said much about war, although his attitude toward one's enemies was far from militant. Matthew 5:10: "Blessed are the peacemakers, for they will be called the sons of God." Matthew 5:43: "You have heard that it was said, 'Love your neighbor and hate your enemy.' But I tell you: Love your enemies and pray for those who persecute you." In Luke 6:27-29: "But I tell you who hear me: Love your enemies, do good to those who hate you, bless those who curse you, pray for those who mistreat you. If someone strikes you on one cheek, turn to him the other also. If someone takes your cloak, do not stop him from taking your tunic."

Vietnamese Buddhist monk Thich Nhat Hahn spoke for many of the stationmasters, regardless of their faith. He said, "Preparing for war and fighting a war means allowing our human nature to die and the animal nature in us to take over." President Dwight D. Eisenhower said something similar: "How far can you go without destroying from within what you are trying to defend from without?" Each person in the network was dedicated to helping war resisters hold on to their humanity.

Faith is a motivating factor for many in the network. Atheists, agnostics, Christians, Jews, Muslims, Quakers, Taoists, even Unitarians, all work together. They break the law to follow what their consciences dictate. Perhaps that's the highest form of devotion: to obey God or conscience rather than man. It's easy to obey one's conscience when it costs nothing. Only sincere belief will allow one to risk negative consequences to follow one's conscience. Conscience unifies the diverse stationmasters.

There are people of conscience north of the border. Four of the Canadians involved in the network are Dr. Bob Woollard, Martin Rossander, Rose Marie Cipryk and Jef Keighley.

Dr. Bob Woollard opposed the American war in Vietnam during the sixties. "There were unacceptable happenings in the world and we had an obligation to do something about it," he said. That obligation continues today. "We have to make a difference," he said. "What is happening is unacceptable. . . . I have some obligation to be available and at the very least be an advocate for the people that need the system and provide the services I can myself."

Part of the problem is fear and its paralyzing effect on the American people. "If you build a big enough bogeyman in your closet you don't have to worry about the fact that your neighbor's hungry or that the roof of your own house is leaking," Woollard said. Fear drove people into inactivity and hopelessness.

Fear also caused what Woollard called a "victim mentality"—more specifically, an attitude of "We are victims and thereby we have no responsibility to express our humanity."

"Huge numbers of countries have suffered far greater and not wreaked the kind of havoc on human rights, the economy and the use of military might that the United States has wreaked," he said. "It's usually those that suffer the least that take the most liberties to wear their suffering on their sleeve and make others suffer."

He believes other countries, especially those critical of the conduct of American troops, should do more to help war resisters. "If you're going to give people advice about the unacceptability of their actions, you have to provide alternatives. That's especially true if by following your advice they put themselves in danger."

Individuals also have a duty to help. "Each of us have an obligation in our own small way to reduce the suffering of those who are brave enough to stand up and refuse to make others suffer through their actions as soldiers," he said. "There's a chain of suffering that has to be broken on a number of levels."

Martin Rossander said he's been an activist since "before there was a word to describe it". The eighty-something-year-old man aided war resisters during the Vietnam War by offering housing and sponsorship. He offers assistance to war resisters today. "This is how change happens, a few people working here and there," he said.

The border is tight now, and it is harder to legally emigrate to Canada than it was during the Vietnam War. Rossander believes the United States will reinstate the draft. Noting that many people enlist in the American military to get ahead in life, he summed up his sentiments in one word: "Exploitation."

Rose Marie Cipryk said helping "just fell to me." She said aiding war resisters is consistent with her pacifist beliefs. She knows of about a dozen others who have offered to shelter war resisters, and at least forty who have offered financial support to Brandon Hughey. She believes that the U.S. is acting "opportunistic in a destructive manner."

"Military incursion is not going to bring peace," she said. "As long as you've got military force, you're going to have an uprising."

Jef Keighley is a union activist opposed to the American war in Iraq. He is setting up a national network of peace activists at www.stopwar.ca. This network will help war resisters.

"Anyone who has come to realize that the war machine needs to be undermined, stopped or reversed is deserving of assistance," Keighley said. "People are demonstrating their conscience not to kill and oppress people, and that's good. [The war] is morally wrong, it's legally wrong, it's a violation of the U.S. Constitution, it's a violation of the Geneva Convention."

The network will offer legal assistance. It will also help war resisters find housing, employment and support.

The lawyer representing two of the deserters is Jeffry House, a draft resister. He left for Canada shortly after he received his draft notice.

"I did not believe the United States had a right to intervene in a foreign civil war," he said in an e-mail interview. "I thought the South Vietnamese government had little homegrown support, and was essentially the creature of the U.S. government, and its predecessor colonial government, France. I believed that the people who were trying to expel the U.S. Forces were basically nationalists, and communists only in a secondary way. I believed that they had a right to select Ho Chi Minh to rule them."

So why did he run? "I did not think it was useful to go to jail," he wrote. "Anyway, I had no desire to be subjected to ill treatment because of my political views. Living in Canada seemed far preferable to jail, and I do not seek martyrdom."

Perhaps this is the mentality of the war resisters.

House worked odd jobs, then went to graduate school and law school. He said people who fled the draft on conscience were generally welcomed with open arms. He decided to help Jeremy Hinzman, the first American deserter to request asylum, then Brandon Hughey and other deserters.

"I think their stand is a brave one, and also one which highlights some of the evil elements of the Iraq War," House wrote. "In my view, anything which is done to end that war will result in fewer Americans

CARL RISING-MOORE AND BECKY OBERG

maimed and killed. Neither Brandon nor Jeremy will kill others in this war, because it does not have a defensive character, nor does it help end terrorism. Their stand is a solid one, and I am pleased to support it."

What is their strategy? "We are arguing in essence that no soldier has an obligation to obey an illegal order. The order to attack and occupy Iraq violates the U.N. Charter and much other international law. The U.S. government threatens those who wish to comply with this law with prison terms. This is persecution.

"We will also have a political strategy in case the court decisions do not favor us. Most Canadians dislike the war, and understand the impulse to avoid it. We hope to intervene in this election to move our government to an openly protective stance."

The War Resisters Support Campaign, a group of prominent Canadians, has demanded that the government offer a special amnesty to "war objectors." The New Democratic Party and Green Party expressed support of this proposal in a questionnaire by the Canadian Peace Alliance. The Liberals have stated they will support international law regarding refugees.

> *5/27/2004*
> *7:47 a.m.*
> *From: Carl Rising-Moore*
> *To: Becky Oberg*

> *The Nuremberg International Military Tribunal from 1945 to 1946 created an important benchmark in the body of the international rule of law, or commonly and historically referred to as the Laws of War.*

> *One of my mentors was Ben Metcalfe. He covered the Nuremberg trials following WWII for the British Foreign Office and the lessons learned there were offered to me as we traveled to the Hat Creek Survival Gathering in British Columbia, Canada, many years ago. Ben impressed upon me the importance of how private citizens, soldiers and companies have a right and duty to disobey their country if they feel their country is breaking the international rules set forth in the*

Nuremberg principles.

These principles offer the world a clear and unambiguous guideline to proceed into the future. No longer could a citizen, soldier or company say, "I could do nothing; I was only following the orders of my leaders." It would be necessary for each and every person in a nation to disobey their leaders if they believed that those orders were immoral and illegal. The greatest crime against humanity would be preemptive war. If many refused to cooperate with their nation, it would be difficult for any country to invade another sovereign state. From a domestic perspective, the bumper sticker during the Vietnam War "My Country, Right or Wrong" would become obsolete and incorrect according to those principles.

The phrase "America—love it or leave it" should be replaced by "America—love it or change it." When I became a naturalized American citizen, I pledged in a videotaped ceremony to become a loyal American. When I read the Constitution, my responsibility seems clear. It is up to me to ensure my country follows a path based on the rule of law and every generation must ensure the correct path of our country both domestically and internationally. In short, I have a duty and right to question the authority of decisions made by elected officials on my behalf.

Post-Nuremberg, sanctions could be imposed upon an entire nation for adopting the Hitler Doctrine of preemptive strike upon another nation.

The Nuremberg International Military Tribunal was a long time coming. There had been numerous attempts to limit the atrocities of war throughout human history with very little success.

Some of the attempts to limit the horror of war were established as a result of World War II and other horrible wars, such as the Geneva Convention (which troops are required to study in basic training). However, the attempts to create Laws of War failed to offer punishment to those nations that disobeyed those laws. For example, after WWI, the Kaiser was allowed to retire to a castle in Holland to live comfortably for the remainder of his life, even though he was responsible for the deaths of millions of people throughout Europe and beyond. The current Laws of War of that period *were insufficient to bring him to trial and the political will did not exist.*

Telford Taylor, the chief prosecutor at the Nuremberg trials, stated in his book <u>The Anatomy of the Nuremberg Trials</u>: "The Nuremberg which is remembered and invoked today is Nuremberg as a source and test of the international law of war. While there are many who deny Nuremberg's validity as a source, they are far outweighed by the nations, international institutions, and people who have accepted Nuremberg's validity or at least look to it for precedent and guidance. There are no permanently established means of enforcing the Nuremberg principles, and they are often flouted, but as a moral and legal statement, clothed with judicial precedent and United Nations recognition, the Nuremberg principles are an international legal force to be reckoned with."

When the Reagan administration was found guilty at the International Criminal Court (ICC) of breaking the principles established at Nuremberg by mining the harbors of Nicaragua, Reagan simply ignored the ICC, which diminished that court's credibility. It was as though a parent said, "Do as I say, not as I do."

When the United States decided to impose the Bush Doctrine of preventive war in its military invasion against Iraq, that act damaged the credibility of the United Nations. When it became clear that the Bush administration could not win a favorable vote in the U.N. Security Council, George W. Bush decided to attack regardless of that failure. Hence the Bush Doctrine was born.

By disregarding the Security Council, the Bush II administration is now vulnerable to a successful criminal prosecution of the United States of America because of that attack upon a sovereign, albeit corrupt, nation. Most Americans will feel very uncomfortable being linked with Hitler's WWII, but this is the reality under international rule of law as set forth by Nuremberg.

Even as the Bush II administration was making plans to Iraq, the administration was attempting to obtain immunity from the ICC to prevent criminal charges being introduced into that court. These legal issues are understood by most nations and are at the heart of the resentment felt on a global scale against the USA.

Even those nations that joined "the Coalition of the Willing" are having problems at home as each participating nation's majority of citizens are today opposed to this illegal and immoral war in Iraq. The citizens of those countries are obeying the Nuremberg Principles, even if their countries are not. Those citizens of the world have been referred to as a superpower as their influence is growing every day. There is no common language, creed, or culture, but what unites this growing superpower is an intuitive understanding that preemptive war is wrong.

As history unfolds, it is doubtful if the USA will be successful in launching similar strikes as "the Coalition of the Willing" is shrinking as I write these words.

No one likes the big bully on the block. Historically, every bully government fails as a result of internal corruption, external opposition, and the final determiner—the cost of maintaining such a vast military-industrial complex.

On May 19, 2004, the United States withdrew

their resolution to renew Resolution 1487, which would renew Resolution 1422. This resolution seeks to exempt the U.S. military in UN peacekeeping forces from arrest and removal for trial at the International Criminal Court in The Hague.

Chapter 4

The Behemoth

"We Americans have no commission from God to police the world."
—President Benjamin Harrison

Have you ever heard of Operation Northwoods? Documents recently released under the Freedom of Information Act reveal a plan that raises interesting and disturbing questions about how far our government will go to justify a war. Would the government fabricate a reason for war, or evidence for war? James Bamford, the author of *Body of Secrets*, the idea was seriously considered.

According to Bamford, President Eisenhower told his chairman of the Joint Chiefs of Staff, Lyman L. Lemnitzer, that he would move against Castro if the Cubans gave him justification. Failing that, perhaps the United States "could think of manufacturing something that would be generally acceptable." Bamford writes: "What he was suggesting was a pretext—a bombing, an attack, an act of sabotage—carried out secretly against the United States *by* the United States. Its purpose would be to justify the launching of a war. It was a dangerous suggestion by a desperate president."

There were numerous suggestions for a pretext. Friendly Cubans, disguised as Cuban soldiers, could start riots near the main gate of the U.S. Navy base at Guantanamo Bay. Friendly Cubans could also pretend to be saboteurs—blowing up ammunition, starting fires, sabotaging aircraft, firing mortars at installations. One was reminiscent of the *USS Maine* explosion in 1898; the Americans could blow up a U.S. ship in Guantanamo Bay and blame Cuba, a national wave of indignation supplied by the casualty list.

"Operation Northwoods called for a war in which many patriotic Americans and innocent Cubans would die senseless deaths—all to satisfy the egos of twisted generals back in Washington, safe in their taxpayer-financed homes and limousines," writes Bamford. The generals proposed sinking a boatload of Cubans en route to Florida, attempt to kill refugees who'd already arrived "safe" in America, "discovering" Cuban weapons and plots in the Dominican Republic, even falsify a plane attack.

Lemnitzer and the Joint Chiefs, some of whom were members of the extreme right-wing John Birch Society, suggested a "terror campaign," bombings, false arrests and hijackings. Lemnitzer believed "the United States can undertake military intervention without the risk of a general war." He believed that "continued police action would be required." He wanted his plan executed "as soon as possible and preferably before the release of National Guard and Reserve forces presently on active duty."

Bamford writes: "The Gulf of Tonkin seems right out of the Operation Northwoods playbook: We could blow up a U.S. ship in Guantanamo Bay and blame Cuba. . . . casualty lists in U.S. newspapers would cause a helpful wave of indignation". One need only replace "Guantanamo Bay" with "Tonkin Gulf" and "Cuba" with "North Vietnam." The Gulf of Tonkin incident may or may not have been stage-managed, but the senior Pentagon leadership at the time was clearly capable of such deceit.

Is the Pentagon leadership still capable of such deceit?

In April 2004, an Iranian news agency reported that American troops had been seen unloading components of weapons of mass destruction. The plan, the reporters alleged, was to construct WMD and hide them in Red Cross containers (a war crime). American media never mentioned the story, not even to denounce it. Would the United States plant weapons of mass destruction in Iraq in order to justify the war? We may never know.

Justification for the Iraq war seems to be changing. First, a reason was that Iraq had and was ready to use weapons of mass destruction. If that were so, why weren't the WMD used during the invasion? In his State of the Union address, Bush said that Saddam Hussein had attempted to buy uranium from Niger, even though the CIA had removed this accusation from another speech months earlier. This charge was proven to be false. The WMD charge has shifted to Iraq had programs to create weapons of mass destruction. That is not the same thing.

Second, there was the claim that Iraq supported al-Qaeda. On his speech on the deck of the *USS Abraham Lincoln*, Bush said Iraq was "an ally of al-Qaeda"—an absurd charge. Saddam Hussein and Osama bin Laden are mortal enemies. Hussein, a secular leader, ruthlessly persecuted members of the Wahabbi sect, which is practiced by bin Laden. In one tape-recorded speech, bin Laden encouraged the people of Iraq to revolt. Al-Qaeda is in Iraq now because we were in Iraq first, not because Saddam Hussein invited them there.

Third, we were liberating the Iraqi people. How does that justify Abu Gharib? Why did we shut down a newspaper for printing anti-Coalition views? Why have we asked Qatar to rein in al-Jazerra? Why are we so slow to allow direct elections? Why do we have so much power after the largely ceremonial June 30 transfer of sovereignty?

Fourth, it was a vital campaign in the War on Terror. However, a CIA study before the invasion said attacking Iraq would *increase* the risk of terrorist attack. How can we fight terrorism by increasing the risk of an attack?

What, then, is the reason for the war?

Is it an inevitable part of American militarism? How many countries does the United States have a military presence in? According to the 2002 Department of Defense publication "Active Duty Military Personnel Strengths by Regional Area and by Country," the United States has troops in 135 countries—in other words, 70 percent of the world's countries. Those countries are:

1. Afghanistan
   --Coalition member

2. Albania
   --Coalition member

3. Algeria

4. Antigua

5. Argentina

6. Azerbaijan
   --Coalition member

7. Australia
   --Coalition member,
   has refused to send
   more troops to Iraq

8. Austria

9. Bahamas

10. Bahrain

11. Bangladesh

12. Barbados

13. Belgium

14. Belize

15. Bolivia

16. Bosnia and Herzegovina

17. Botswana

18. Brazil

19. Bulgaria
    --Coalition member

20. Burma
    (also known as
    Myanmar)

21. Burundi

22. Cambodia

23. Cameroon

24. Canada

25. Chad

26. Chile

27. China
    (including Hong Kong)

28. Columbia
    --Coalition member

29. Congo
    (capital Braazaville)

30. Congo
    (formerly Zaire,
    capital Kinsasha)

31. Costa Rica

32. Cote D'Ivoire
    (formerly Ivory Coast)

33. Cuba

34. Cyprus

35. Czech Republic

36. Denmark
--Coalition member

37. Djibouti

38. Dominican Republic
--withdrew all
troops from Iraq

39. East Timor

40. Ecuador

41. Egypt

42. El Salvador
--Coalition member

43. Eritrea
--Coalition member

44. Estonia
--Coalition member

45. Ethiopia
--Coalition member

46. Fiji

47. Finland

48. France

49. Georgia
(A republic that was
part of the former
Soviet Union.)

--Coalition member

50. Germany

51. Ghana

52. Greece

53. Guatemala
--The CIA overthrew
a democratically
elected government in
1954. Forty years of
atrocities followed.

54. Guinea

55. Haiti

56. Honduras
--withdrew all
troops from Iraq

57. Hungary
--Coalition member

58. Iceland

59. India

60. Indonesia
(including Timor)

61. Iraq

62. Israel

63. Italy
--Coalition member

64. Jamaica

65. Japan
    --Coalition member

66. Jordan

67. Kazakhstan

68. Kenya

69. Kuwait

70. Kyrgyzstan

71. Laos

72. Latvia

73) Lebanon
    --In *9-11*, Noam Chomsky reports that in 1985, the Reagan administration detonated a truck bomb outside a mosque. The bomb exploded as people were leaving; 80 were killed and 250 were wounded. Most were women and children. The target, a cleric, survived. Many believe that the suicide bombing of a barracks in 1983 was the U.S's first battle with terrorism by Muslim extremists.

74. Liberia

75. Lithuania

76. Luxembourg

77. Macedonia
    --Coalition member

78. Madagascar

79. Malawi

80. Mali

81. Malaysia

82. Malta

83. Mexico

84. Mongolia

85. Morocco

86. Mozambique

87. Nepal

88. Netherlands (also called Holland)
    --Coalition member

89. New Zealand

90. Nicaragua
--Coalition member, successfully sued the U.S. in the World Court for terrorism

91. Niger

92. Nigeria

93. North Korea

94. Norway

95. Oman

96. Pakistan

97. Paraguay

98. Peru

99. Philippines
--Coalition member

100. Poland
--Coalition member, complained about deceit used to justify war

101. Portugal

102. Qatar

103. Romania
--Coalition member

104. Russia

105. Saudi Arabia

106. Senegal

107. Serbia and Montenegro (includes Kosovo)

108. Singapore

109. Sierra Leone

110. Slovenia

111. Spain
--Coalition member, withdrew all troops from Iraq

112. South Africa

113. South Korea

114. Sri Lanka

115. Suriname

116. Syria

117. Sweden

118. Switzerland

119. Tanzania

120. Thailand

121. Togo

122. Trinidad and Tobago

123. Tunisia
124. Turkey
    --Coalition member
125. Turkmenistan
126. Uganda
127. Ukraine
128. United Arab Emirates
129. United Kingdom
    --Coalition member

130. Uruguay
131. Venezuela
132. Vietnam
133. Yemen
134. Zambia
135. Zimbabwe

The average American will have difficulty locating most of these countries on a map. The average American may not have even heard of some of these countries. That's the current scope of American military presence worldwide.

"The Department of Defense should be renamed the Department of Offense," said Carl.

In his book *A Pretext for War*, James Bamford criticizes Bush for not defying his security and immediately returning to Washington. He compares Bush's 9/11 response to Lyndon B. Johnson's response to the Kennedy assassination. Johnson was sworn in on the plane, flew straight to Washington, and gave a speech at Andrews Air Force Base. Bush could have easily overridden the recommendations of his security advisers, ordered Cheney to report to a secret location, and returned to Andrews Air Force Base to give a defiant speech. "That would have been the courageous thing to do," Bamford writes. Instead, Bush hid while Cheney remained in the White House. Bush did not return until his security advisers were sure Washington was safe.

Continuation of Government—COG—was a postapocalyptic plan originally drafted by President Eisenhower. "We would have to run this country as one big camp—severely regimented," he instructed his advisers. Martial law would be implemented and many civil liberties suspended. He designated eight private citizens to find their way to the center of power after a nuclear attack, where they would take over one of the emergency government functions.

The Kennedy government discovered this plan by accident. What he did with this knowledge is unknown.

After the failed assassination attempt of Ronald Reagan, a plan known as the Presidential Successor Support System was developed. According to Bamford, Vice President George H.W. Bush and Lieutenant Colonel Oliver North were to be given overall responsibility for this new shadow government, which was hidden in the "National Program Office". Bamford does not report whether they knew they were to be given this responsibility. Key players, according to Bamford, included a Congressman from Wyoming named Dick Cheney, CEO of G.D. Searle & Co. (makers of Nutra-Sweet) Donald Rumsfeld, and private lawyer James Woolsey. Unlike Eisenhower, however, Reagan's backup team included a president. George H.W. Bush continued the blatantly unconstitutional program, but Bill Clinton ended it.

Bamford writes: "The existence of the secret government was so closely held that Congress was completely bypassed. Rather than through legislation, it was created by Top Secret presidential fiat. In fact, Congress would have no role in the new wartime administration. 'One of the awkward questions we faced,' said one of the participants, 'was whether to reconstitute Congress after a nuclear attack. It was decided that no, it would be easier to operate without them.'"

Bamford reports that George W. Bush decided to reinstate part of the plan on September 11. Only Vice President Cheney and very few in the executive branch were notified. The Speaker of the House Dennis Hastert (R-Ill.) and president pro tempore of the Senate Robert C. Byrd (D-W.Va.), the officials who by law are first and second in the line of succession after the vice president, were not notified.

Democracy in Iraq? Carl shakes his head and suggests we need democracy in America first.

Freedom Underground

Chapter 5

The Conductor

"When people speak to you about a preventive war, you tell them to go fight it. After my experience, I have come to hate war." —Dwight D. Eisenhower

Carl's paternal grandfather, Arthur Rising, was in the infantry in the Canadian Army during World War I. He was killed by a hand grenade in the trenches of France. The children were sent to an orphanage, and the Moore family adopted Carl's father, Frederick. In keeping with a British tradition, he hyphenated his given name and adopted name. Hence, Dr. Frederick Rising-Moore.

Frederick served in World War II. He spent six years in the Canadian Army, and saw action in North Africa and Italy. He was a communications commando, which meant his unit engaged the enemy, reported their position to headquarters, and escaped.

Carl's mother, Kathleen, was in the British Royal Air Force as a photographer. She survived the Battle of Britain. Carl's brother, Rick, was born during the battle, and his mother held him up to the window as the bombs fell so he would remember what the war was about.

"We're military all the way back," said Carl. His ancestors were involved in the Norman invasion of England.

Rick Rising-Moore served in the U.S. Army Corps of Engineers as a bulldozer operator. He helped build the "Freedom Highway" in Thailand.

On September 16, 1964, Carl Rising-Moore was sworn in for a three-year term. Although he was a Canadian citizen, he was eligible for the draft. He wanted to volunteer for the draft and serve two years, but the induction sergeant told him the military had done away with that. Eager to fight communists, Carl agreed to the three-year term and was assigned the service number RA 16815719.

When he was shipped by bus to Ft. Knox for basic training, he asked his seatmate, "Are you regular Army or drafted?" When his seatmate replied he'd volunteered for the draft, Carl was furious. The military had lied to him! The first sergeant at Ft. Knox said it was too late to change and volunteer for the draft; he'd already signed his contract.

He was made an acting corporal and served as a squad leader during basic. His scores were high in overall proficiency. "I was a pretty gung ho soldier," he said.

A soldier in an adjacent company committed suicide during Basic. Carl helped another soldier learn how to assemble and disassemble his weapon, but the frustrated soldier banged his fist against the barracks floor. Carl realized he was not emotionally stable and realized there was virtually no screening of who fought. "I always wondered if he made it or not," Carl said.

Shortly after those incidents, he had a nightmare. The military was trying to steal his spirit. He woke up in a cold sweat, and then began thinking.

His father had told him about the Canadian military, which strived to train soldiers. The United States military, however, tried to break people. He remembered a lecture his company had heard—they could face a general court-martial and be shot for refusing to fight in battle. "You may survive by going after the enemy," the speaker said, "but if you refuse we can kill you."

After basic, he was assigned to administration school at Ft. Knox. He was in the top of his class, so he was sent to finance school at Ft. Benjamin Harrison in Indianapolis. After finishing finance school, he was assigned to Hanau, Germany, in the 2nd Support Brigade Headquarters for the Third Army.

The journey was by troop ship. Carl referred to it as "the most disgusting trip I've ever taken in my whole life." Many of the soldiers had never been on a ship before, and became seasick. There was a constant stench of vomit. When he arrived in Hanau, he was assigned to work on the temporary duty fund. It was here he would commit his first political act. He was eighteen.

He realized that much of the temporary duty fund was used to finance "temporary duty" in Munich during the Oktoberfest and other European parties.

Disturbed at this abuse of the fund, he asked a lieutenant what to do. The lieutenant discussed the issue with members of the Army Security Agency (ASA) at the officers' club, and then told Carl he could probably get away with changing the practice. Carl waited until a despised officer, a major, demanded temporary duty fund. Carl rejected the funding, citing an Army regulation that required the major to sign out and sign in on a morning report. This would leave a record of where the major was.

The enraged major remarked, "What the hell kind of Army is this?!" and demanded to know what right a private had to deny a major temporary duty funding.

Carl replied, "With all due respect, sir, these Army Regulations are signed by the general of the Army, and he clearly outranks you." The major stormed off to get a colonel. A sergeant major asked what was going on and told Carl the brigade commander wanted to talk to him.

The brigade commander rebuked Carl. Carl bluffed and replied that he'd written a report and sent it to his girlfriend, with the instructions to hand-deliver it to the general of the Army unless she heard from him. The brigade commanded demanded to know when he had sent it and from what mailbox. Carl replied he'd sent it the previous week. The brigade commander restricted Carl to his barracks and ordered him not to speak to anyone.

A legal staff captain came over to Carl's barracks and asked what was going on. Carl explained the situation, and the captain and went over to talk to the brigade commander. Carl waited outside while the two officers talked. The brigade commander was up for promotion to brigadier general and about to retire. In civilian life, a general could join the board of directors of a company as a figurehead and receive a generous, lifelong stipend that could equal or exceed military retirement pay.

Suddenly, the brigade commander came to Carl. "Son, what are you doing as an enlisted man?" he asked, smiling. He told Carl he should consider Officer Candidate School, and that he would fast track him to the rank of Specialist Fourth Class. He told him to run the temporary duty fund as he saw fit. Carl did so and cut the fund by 75 percent by the next quarter. A colonel later came by his office and said, "I just want to shake your hand, sir."

"People either loved me or hated me," said Carl. Either way, he was convinced he could speak the truth to power.

Carl had joined to fight, and he volunteered for combat duty in Vietnam. His request was denied. After he was promoted to specialist, he was reassigned to Ft. Bragg, North Carolina, on twenty-four hours' notice. It was late 1966. He was assigned to the Training Center, where due to a backlog he spent twelve to fourteen hours a day working on payroll problems. He joined the 101st Airborne Parachute Club, and befriended several returning Special Forces soldiers. Everyone who had been to Vietnam was "whacked out."

"This war wasn't all it was knocked out to be," Carl said.

One day, Carl and a Special Forces soldier went on a jump together. "I jumped first and was on the ground while the airplane circled higher and higher," Carl said. "At about 7,000 feet he jumped. He was the last to jump, and we all watched as he dropped below 2,000 feet. Then 1,000 feet. Then 500 feet. We were all screaming at him 'Pull! Pull!' He pulled about 200 feet, swung once and landed. When he walked over to us, I could see his eyes were glazed and he was walking like a zombie. I asked him what was on his mind, and he just shrugged his shoulders."

Carl wrote "In reality, the horror of what they were involved in in 'Nam had created walking time bombs. These battle-scarred men and a draftee who explained the draft and war in a compelling manner had me doubting the morality and legality of 'Nam."

Disillusioned, Carl told an officer and friend, Captain Clinso Copeland, that he was through with the Army and would rather spend the rest of his enlistment in the stockade than supporting what he considered an immoral war. Copeland, an African American, had been passed over for promotion many times because of his race. Copeland convinced him to carry on and try to change things from the outside.

Carl was honorably discharged in 1967 and has been trying to change things ever since. He writes:

> *Believe my feelings.*
>
> *Every time I have contemplated an act of civil disobedience (CD), most of my friends and associates have tried to talk me out of it. I proceed only because of an inner instinct or feeling that the action is correct. After these same friends and associates are pleased with the results, even though they tried to convince me to not proceed due to*
>
> *a. it is dangerous*
>
> *b. it will undermine the efforts already underway that did not involve CD*
>
> *c. CD will not work*
>
> *d. it will embarrass those close to me*
>
> *e. I could be more effective outside of jail.*
>
> *What they do not understand is that CD can be justified only when all other measures have been exhausted. Only when every other avenue has been exhausted can it be "seen to be justified" and indeed many by that time will be on board with the decision.*

A nonviolent revolutionary must be prepared for criticism. It will come from one's opponent of course, but it will also come from those that you consider your friends and allies. It is that criticism that has the potential to do the most damage. Those closest to you can hurt like no others.

In the end, once the decision has been made to proceed with CD, it is important to stay true to yourself and your decision. You can fail CD, but nonviolent CD will not fail you if you persevere. One must never give up.

CD is an offensive effort that is similar to launching an offensive battle in war. The difference is that those launching CD are not risking the lives of their opponent but rather the risk is to oneself. Mahatma Gandhi and Dr. Martin Luther King never threatened the safety or person of their opponent. The risk was instead upon themselves.

Gandhi said, "Nonviolence is the weapon of the brave." Indeed, when one engages CD, it is no longer nonviolent if it endangers the public safety. That fact escapes many that employ CD as a tactic. Only when CD considers the public safety can CD be considered nonviolent.

This does not mean that violence will not happen,

but that violence will only be directed toward the nonviolent soldier. If innocent people are injured as a result of an act of CD, it can no longer be considered nonviolent.

Henry David Thoreau gave us "the duty of civil disobedience." It took many decades for Gandhi to discover Thoreau and apply the principle of nonviolence, hence nonviolent civil disobedience was born.

My belief is that this form of warfare has the potential to reverse the age-old drift toward an increasingly violent world. The discovery of nuclear weapons and the use of these weapons on Nagasaki and Hiroshima demonstrated to the world that warfare must end as a mechanism for international problem solving. Differences will still exist, but these debates must end by engaging diplomacy versus war. Indeed, war is a result of failed diplomacy and in many instances diplomacy was undermined by an aggressive foreign policy that had no intention of avoiding war.

Gandhi's Peace Brigades is a concept that has yet to be fully tested. The formation of such brigades to reduce tension in potential conflict was contemplated by Gandhi *before his assassination. The irony that the Kashmir is considered today the most likely "trigger" of a nuclear weapons exchange between India and Pakistan is ironic. The Kashmir is the area that Gandhi was about to visit to organize his Peace Brigades. To this day, that area remains the world's most important location for a concentrated effort to reduce the tension between those two countries.*

The decision by the USA to invade Afghanistan following 9/11, which elevated the criminal acts of terrorists to the level of statehood, will go down in history as a benchmark in failed diplomacy. Instead of engaging the International Criminal Court, the USA has decided that as the so-called sole superpower, it has the right and duty to launch this never-ending "War on Terror." As a result, the USA has lost the goodwill of all nations. Even those nations that joined the USA in this "War on Terror" have discovered that the populations of those individual countries are predominately opposed to the aggressive "Bush Doctrine" of preemptive war. Indeed, the world now has become a much more dangerous place as a result of that doctrine.

The Nuremberg principles that became the international precedent against the preemptive war by Hitler was ignored by the Bush administration. Instead, we have a group of extreme right-wing ideologues that have destabilized our entire planet and increased the incidence of terrorist attacks.

Chapter 6

Bush—Did He Desert?

Following is the result of exhaustive research into Bush's military record. It is important to examine his record considering the purpose of the Freedom Underground. Bush, as commander in chief, sets the standard for all military personnel. A true leader never asks his or her subordinates to do something he or she wouldn't do. Yet that's exactly what Bush has been doing: He is asking our troops to do something he did not do.

"The other reality of the spring of 1968 was Vietnam. The war became increasingly personal as friends who had graduated the year before went into the military. The war was no longer something that was happening to other people in a distant land; it came home to us," Bush wrote.

Yale senior George W. Bush rarely spoke of Vietnam, although the war was on the minds of many of his friends. Their student deferments would expire once they graduated college. Each person had to decide what to do. Bush's father and grandfather both supported the war.

Many wanted to avoid going overseas. James Lockhart II, a Bush classmate, said "Our parents had been in the military, and it was just something that was accepted. . . . The Army was not the spot to end up. . . . The general opinion was to get into a branch of the service that if you'd be sent to Vietnam you had to volunteer to get there rather than just be sent."

Bush registered with Texas Local Board No. 62 in downtown Houston. He talked with his summertime friends about the alternatives after his deferment would expire. Bush's friend Doug Hannah said "George and I used to talk all the time that there has to be a better alternative than being a lieutenant in the Army. We didn't know people who were killed in

Vietnam. We lost more friends to motorcycle accidents than we ever did to Vietnam."

Bush, as a Congressman's son, was in little danger. In her book *Long Time Passing: Vietnam and the Haunted Generation*, Myra MacPherson reported that 234 sons of senators and congressmen came of age during U.S. involvement of the Vietnam War. Of that 234, only 28 served in Vietnam. Of that group, only 19 "saw combat," circumstances undescribed. Only one was wounded. Six senators' sons flunked their physicals (Molly Ivins and Lou Dubose, *Shrub: The Short But Happy Political Life of George W. Bush* 8).

Compare these 234 to the less fortunate men in Project 100,000, an almost-forgotten Great Society program. Every year, 100,000 men who were previously rejected for military service were rehabilitated and inducted. These recruits were derisively nicknamed "the Moron Squad," and were mostly poor Southern and black youth. Forty-one percent of the soldiers in the program were African American, compared to 12 percent in the Army as a whole. Forty percent were trained for combat, compared with 25 percent of the services in general. Project 100,000 had a killed-in-action ratio almost exactly twice as high as other units'. The Army accepted recruits with IQs as low as 62. Under federal law, a mentally retarded inmate—i.e., one with an IQ of 62—cannot be executed.

Although speakers came to campus to talk about the war, Bush and his friends did not attend. "I knew I would serve," he writes. "Leaving the country to avoid the draft was not an option for me; I was too conservative and too traditional. My inclination was to support the government and the war until proven wrong, and that only came later, as I realized we could not explain the mission, had no exit strategy, and did not seem to be fighting to win."

Bush decided to be a fighter pilot. He investigated the Texas Air National Guard. He took his pilot aptitude test at Westover Air Force Base in Massachusetts in January 1968. That May, he met with Colonel William "Buck" Staudt and was accepted. He enlisted twelve days before his graduation, ensuring his return to Texas. Bush said, "I was not prepared to shoot my eardrum out with a shotgun in order to get a deferment. Nor was I willing to go to Canada. I decided to better myself by learning how to fly airplanes. . . I don't want to play like I was somebody out there marching when I wasn't. It was either Canada or the service and I was headed into the service. Somebody said the Guard was looking for pilots. All I know is there weren't many people trying to be pilots."

His claim is debatable. According to Texas Guard historians, there were ninety-eight officer slots authorized for Bush's unit, seventy-two of which were full. Of the twenty-six remaining slots, five were set aside for pilots. These slots were assigned according to age, applicant's education level, and test scores. Some Guard officials claim there was a waiting list. Major General Thomas Bishop, who was the state's adjutant general, said the unit was full. Retired chief caster cergeant Joe Briggs said, "There was a five hundred-man waiting list prior to 1972, so there was not much recruiting. When someone left, you went to the next guy in line."

Former speaker of the Texas House Ben Barnes

acknowledged that he sometimes received requests for help in obtaining Guard slots. He said he never received such a call from anyone in the Bush family. When asked if an intermediary or friend of the family had asked him to intercede on Bush's behalf, he declined to comment. "I had a lot of requests," he said. "With the National Guard being an agency of the state of Texas, it was obviously helpful for the governor, lieutenant governor and the speaker to be recommending you."

Barnes' aide, Nick Kralj, simultaneously served as aide to Brigadier General James M. Rose, head of the Texas Air National Guard. Kralj admitted in a deposition he would get calls from Barnes or Barnes' chief of staff, "saying so-and-so is interested in getting in the Guard." Kralj said he forwarded the names to General Rose. Kralj said he could not recall any of the names he gave to Rose (Lardner). Barnes testified under oath that he pulled strings to get Bush into the Guard (Begala).

Some described it as an underground railroad.

On May 27, 1968, Bush was sworn in as an airman.

His commander, Colonel Walter B. "Buck" Staudt, staged a special ceremony so he could be photographed swearing Bush in, rather than the captain who swore him in. The National Guard was aware Bush was a congressman's son, and they used him several times for public relations purposes.

Bush signed a statement of intent. He promised, after graduating pilot training, "to return to my unit and fulfill my obligation to the utmost of my ability." He also stated "I have applied for pilot training with the goal of making flying a lifetime pursuit and I believe I can best accomplish this to my own satisfaction by serving as a member of the Air National Guard as long as possible." He was assigned to the 147th Fighter Group.

Some people called the unit "The Champagne Unit." According to journalist Molly Ivins, the unit included the son of former Texas senator Lloyd Bentsen, the son of former Texas governor John Connally, two sons of Texas businessman Sid Adger (who was identified as the family friend who interceded to get Bush into the Guard) and several members of the Dallas Cowboys football team.

When Bush took the Air Force Officers Qualification Test at Westover Air Force Base in Massachusetts, he scored a 25 percent for pilot aptitude, which was the lowest passing score. He scored 50 percent on navigator aptitude. However, he scored 95 percent on questions designed to reflect "officer quality"—the current average is 88 percent.

Bush did his six weeks of basic training at Lackland Air Force Base in San Antonio. After he was commissioned as a second lieutenant in November of 1968, he got a two-plus-month leave to work on a Senate campaign for Edward J. Gurney. He was on inactive duty status at this time, and occasionally returned to Houston for weekend Guard duty.

Bush's commission was unusual. His military education consisted of basic training and undergraduate pilot training. Normally, commissions were given to people who had eight semesters of ROTC in college, eighteen months of military service, or completion of Air Force officer training school. Texas National Guard historian Tom Hail said he "never heard of that" except for flight surgeons.

His pilot training began in November at Moody Air Force Base in Valdosta, Georgia. Although he was the only Guardsman there, he soon earned his classmates' respect with the way he learned to handle a plane. He spent fifty-five weeks on active duty, graduating in December 1969. His father, who had given the commencement speech, pinned on his second lieutenant wings.

He returned to Houston and, by all accounts, performed hazardous duty honorably. He flew F-102 Delta Daggers; his unit kept two, fully armed, on round-the-clock alert. According to reports, the F-102 "was considered a dinosaur and not an integral part of the armed forces." The F-102s used in Vietnam flew alongside B-52s during combat air patrols and were armed with Falcon missiles (which were nuclear). Military historians have said there was a shortage of F-102 pilots during this time precisely because the plane was obsolete—the military considered it a much higher priority to train pilots for other, more important aircraft. In 1974, the 147th would be one of the last National Guard outfits to retire the plane.

Bush wrote: "Several of my fellow pilots had participated in a program known as 'Palace Alert,' which rotated Guard pilots into Vietnam to relieve active-duty pilots. A friend and fellow pilot, Fred Bradley, and I were interested in participating and we talked with Colonel Jerry Killian about it. He told us the program was being phased out, that a few more pilots would go, but that Fred and I had not logged enough hours to participate."

This statement is both true and misleading. When Bush filled out his enlistment papers, those documents included a question about whether or not the enlistee would volunteer for overseas service. Bush checked that he did not wish to volunteer. Some have speculated that some other, unknown person checked off that box without Bush's knowledge. The more believable explanation is that he was instructed to check that box since he was serving in Texas, not Vietnam.

Tim Russert asked Bush himself whether he "volunteer[ed] or enlist[ed] to go." Bush replied, "No, I didn't." This contrasts with what he wrote in his autobiography. *The Washington Post* found an interesting fact: in 1999, the *Post* discovered that Palace Alert had been shut down one week after Bush got out of flight school. Even had the program not been shut down, Bush had logged only three hundred hours of flight time, which qualified him to fly the F-102 without an instructor but was far short of the five hundred hours of experience required for Palace Alert.

On November 3, 1970, Bush was promoted to 1st lieutenant. He was promoted by Rose.

Bush wrote, "I continued flying with my unit for the next several years." That statement is false. June 1970 to May 1971 would be the last time he fulfilled his obligations. He served forty-six days of flight duty, the expected weekend duty and extra runway standby alert time. By May 1972, he was credited with twenty-two flight duty days, fourteen days short of the minimum thirty-six days he owed the Guard that year. April 1972 also marked the last time he flew in an F-102.

This could have had serious consequences for Bush. He signed a statement stating: "I understand that I may be ordered to active duty for a period not to exceed 24 months for unsatisfactory participation." It was not unusual for Guardsmen and Reservists to be ordered to active duty for missing drills.

On May 15, 1972, Bush cleared the base, according to one of his squadron's supervising officers, Lieutentant Colonel William D. Harris, Jr. On May 24, Bush was in Alabama, and he requested in writing a six-month transfer to an inactive Reserve postal unit. He was in Alabama to work on the Senate campaign of Republican Winton M. "Red" Blout. Although this unit had no airplanes, his commanders approved the request. On May 31, 1972, National Guard Bureau headquarters denied the request. This would obligate him to his Houston unit, but he remained in Alabama.

On September 5, 1972, Bush was granted a three-month transfer to do his Guard duty with the 187th Tactical Region Group of the Alabama Air Guard. Here the record becomes unclear. His military records do not show any duty in Alabama, and, according to several witnesses, Bush never showed up.

The commanding officer, General William Turnipseed, said Bush never showed. "Had he reported in, I would have had some recall, and I do not. I had been in Texas, done my flight training there. If we had had a first lieutenant from Texas, I would have remembered." Turnipseed later backed away from this statement and gave Bush the benefit of the doubt.

The general's administrative officer, Kenneth K. Lott, says he has no recollection of Bush reporting for duty. Retired colonel Albert Lloyd, a longtime Texas Air National Guard official and Bush supporter, told *The Boston Globe* he did not know if Bush reported. "If he did, his drill attendance should have been certified and sent to Ellington, and there would have been a record. We cannot find the records to show he fulfilled the requirements in Alabama." More damning, Bush's discharge papers have no record of service whatsoever in Alabama.

Two members of that unit were told to expect him and were looking for him. Both Bob Mintz and Paul Bishop are certain he never showed.

"I remember that I heard someone was coming to drill with us from Texas," Mintz, then a first lieutenant, said in an interview with the *Memphis Flyer*.

"And it was implied that it was somebody with political influence." Mintz said he never saw Bush, "And I was looking for him. . . . There's no way we wouldn't have noticed a strange rooster in the henhouse, especially since we were *looking* for him." Mintz, a former registered Republican who voted for Gore, retired with the rank of lieutenant colonel.

Bishop, also a lieutenant at the time, said, "I never saw hide nor hair of Mr. Bush." Bishop, who voted for Bush in 2000 but leans toward the Democrats in the upcoming election, retired with the rank of colonel. "It bothered me that he wouldn't fess up and say, Okay, guys, I cut out when the rest of you did your time," he said. "He shouldn't have tried to dance around the subject. I take great exception to that. I spent thirty-nine years defending my country."

John B. "Bill" Calhoun said he saw Bush at Dannelly at times during mid-1972. However, the White House acknowledges Bush did not pull Alabama Guard duty at that time. Bush's first drills, according to the White House, were in October. The White House never explained the discrepancy or why so many others said they did not see him, especially after a retired colonel said the unit's hanger was laid out so that it was "virtually impossible" for Bush to have met with Calhoun and for none of the unit's eight hundred other reservists to have seen him.

Dental records show Bush was examined on January 6, 1973, at Dannelly Air National Guard base. This has absolutely nothing to do with whether or not he was attending drills as required. Bush was supposed to be in Texas at this time, as the Senate campaign and his temporary transfer were over.

Something critical happened on September 29, 1972. The National Guard Bureau notified Bush that he had been verbally suspended from flying on August 1, and the written order made it official. "Reason for suspension: failure to accomplish annual medical examination."

This can mean one of two things. One, he did not take his medical examination. Two, he took his medical examination and for some reason failed it. Bush's campaign gave three excuses.

First, they claimed Bush missed the exam because

Bush was in Alabama while his physician was in Houston. The problem: Personal physicians do not perform a military medical examination. A flight surgeon, who has the power to remove pilots from flying status, conducts the examinations. Flight surgeons were on every Air Force base then, so it should have been relatively easy for Bush to find a qualified physician to do the physical. According to Robinson, the physical could have been done at the base in Montgomery.

Second, they claimed his paperwork had not caught up with him. Bush spokesman Dan Bartlett claimed Bush was aware he would be suspended for missing his medical exam, but he had no choice as his transfer had not yet been approved. "It was just a question of following the bureaucratic procedure of the time," said Bartlett. "He knew the suspension would have to take place." This is somewhat plausible, but it raises the question of why Bush did not take care of this before applying for his transfer or after his first transfer request was denied.

Third, they claimed Bush transferred to Alabama as a non-flying Guardsman and therefore did not need to take the physical. However, how can a pilot be performing equivalent duty in a non-flying status? It is not the pilot's decision to fly, nor is it up to the pilot whether or not to take the physical.

Regardless of why he missed the physical, the fact remains that missing a physical usually triggers an investigation, which results in a Flight Inquiry Board being convened. It is considered a serious offense. "There's no excuse for that," said Major General Paul A. Weaver, Jr., who retired as the Pentagon's director of the Air National Guard in 2002. "Aviators just don't miss their physical."

Brigadier General David L. McGinnis concurred. McGinnis said missing the physical violated Bush's pledge to fly for at least five years after completing flight school. "Failure to take your flight physical is like a failure to show up for duty," he said. "It is an obligation you can't blow off."

There is no record of an investigation. McGinnis said there should be an investigation and a report. "If it didn't happen, that shows how far they were willing to stretch the rules to accommodate," he said.

A popular rumor claims that Bush was afraid his

physical, which might have included a drug test, would reveal substance abuse. The Pentagon announced on December 31, 1969, that it would begin random substance abuse tests during physicals. While Bush officials claim he was not aware of any changes that required a drug test, this does not hold up under scrutiny. In 1969, the year after Bush's enlistment, the Pentagon notified every unit in the military that it would implement random drug testing at some point in the near future. When that moment arrived—April 1972—every service member, officer or enlisted, overseas or stateside, would have been aware of this change. The purpose of the random drug tests was to make it absolutely clear to every service member that the Pentagon would not tolerate any substance abuse from anyone.

On the campaign trail in 2000, Bush stated he has not used drugs or alcohol in excess since 1974. This chronology makes it possible that he was abusing substances during his enlistment. He admits he was a hard drinker at the time, and friends said he partied and drank regularly.

It is possible that the Human Reliability Program (HRP) was invoked. The human reliability regulations were used to screen military personnel for mental, physical and emotional fitness before they were granted access to nuclear weapons and delivery systems. In a 1974 Washington Air National Guard case, two airmen were suspended on suspicion of drug use. Both eventually received honorable discharges. Former Air Force briefing officer Marty Isham said there is a "good likelihood" HRP regulations were either applied or about to be applied to Bush, resulting in the suspension.

Regardless of the reason for his "failure to accomplish annual medical examination," there is another question. At the time, the air war in Vietnam was at its height. The Air Force had a shortage of pilots. Was the grounding sufficient punishment for what one pilot described as "a flagrant dereliction of duty."

Bush returned to Texas in the fall of 1972. However, he did not return to his unit. Two special orders commanding Bush to report for nine days of active duty were issued. Bush did not do so. His commanding officers, Harris and Killian, wrote they could not rate his performance for the prior twelve months because he had not been at the unit.

The next record of service is May 29, 1973. Several duty days are also logged in June and July. He spent a total of thirty-six days on duty—the Guard requirements.

July 30, 1973, was the last time Bush wore his uniform. He requested an early discharge. On October 1, 1973, Bush was honorably discharged from the Texas Air National Guard. His scheduled discharge was May 26, 1974. However, his discharge from the inactive Reserves was November 1974. Why the extra six months?

His military career was marked by favoritism. He had excessive absences. Whether he should be considered a deserter depends on how strictly one interprets the regulations. According to the Texas Military Code, "[A] commissioned officer of the state military forces who, after tender of his resignation and before notice of its acceptance, quits his post or proper duties without leave and with intent to remain away permanently is guilty of desertion."

Bush asked for his discharge on September 5, 1973. The discharge was granted on October 1, 1973. Bush was "not available for signature" when his discharge was granted; he had already left for graduate school at Harvard. Some say that by leaving before his discharge was official, he deserted.

It is difficult to go so far as to call Bush a deserter. That said, it is necessary to ask how a man whose military career was distinguished by favoritism and accommodation can ask American service members to make the ultimate sacrifice. What right does he have?

Carl is less forgiving. "It is clear that when the assertation of his AWOL status became a political issue in 2004, the White House stated that they would release proof of his service. After journalists were allowed to study documents at the White House (but prevented from removing those documents), there was general consensus among those journalists that there was no new evidence to prove Bush had not been AWOL."

What did Bush learn from his military experience? He writes: "I also learned the lesson of Vietnam. Our nation should be slow to engage troops. But when we do so, we must do so with ferocity. We must not go into a conflict unless we go in committed to win. We can never again ask the military to fight a political war. If America's strategic interests are at stake, if diplomacy fails, if no other option will accomplish the objective, the Commander in Chief must define the mission and allow the military to achieve it."

I report it without comment.

Timeline of U.S. and Bush Involvement in Vietnam

Nov. 1, 1963	South Vietnamese generals seize power in a U.S.-approved coup.
Nov. 2, 1963	South Vietnamese President Ngo Dinh Diem is assassinated.
Aug. 1964	Gulf of Tonkin incident. North Vietnamese boats fire at the U.S.S. Maddox, a spy ship in North Vietnamese waters. One bullet hits. A few days later, there is another alleged attack. There is no visual confirmation of the attack, although American media grossly distort the facts.
Aug. 7, 1964	Congress passes the Gulf of Tonkin Resolution.
Jan. 17, 1968	George Walker Bush takes Air Force officer and pilot qualification tests. He scores 25, the lowest passing grade, on the pilot aptitude portion. He checks "do not volunteer" for overseas assignments and lists "none" as background qualifications.
March 16, 1968	My Lai massacre. U.S. troops kill more than 300 civilians.

May 1968	Bush graduates from Yale. Half a million troops are fighting in Vietnam; American casualties are about 350 killed each week.
May 27, 1968	Bush is sworn in. Six weeks later, he receives a "special appointment" and commission as a second lieutenant. This normally required eight semesters of college ROTC courses, 18 months of military service, or completion of Air Force officer training school.
Sept. 4, 1968	Bush is commissioned a second lieutenant. He takes an eight-week leave to work on a Senate campaign in Florida.
Nov. 25, 1968–Nov. 28, 1969	Bush attends flight school and logs approximately 300 hours of training flight time. While this allows him to solo, it is short of the 500 hours experience required for volunteer active duty combat operations in Vietnam.

Timeline of U.S. and Bush Involvement in Vietnam

July 1970	Bush earns his wings.
Nov. 3, 1970	Bush is promoted to first lieutenant.
June 1970– May 1971	Bush is credited with 46 days of flight duty.
June 1971– May 1972	Bush is credited with 22 days of flight duty. This is 14 days short of the minimum 36 days that he owed the Guard.
April 1972	Bush's last F-102 flight.
May 15, 1972	Bush clears his base in Texas and moves to Alabama.
May 24, 1972	Bush files a written request for a six-month transfer to an inactive postal Reserve unit.
May 31, 1972	National Guard Bureau headquarters denies the transfer request.
August 1, 1972	Bush grounded for "failure to accomplish annual medical examination."
Sept. 5, 1972	Bush ordered to serve three months in an active but non-flying administrative Guard unit. No official notation shows he reported.

Nov. 19, 1972– Fall 1973	Bush returns to Houston, but not his unit.
Dec. 18– Dec. 29, 1972	Intense "Christmas bombings" of North Vietnam by US. 1,318 civilians killed.
May 2, 1973	The two lieutenant colonels in charge of Bush's unit cannot rate him for the past 12 months, explaining he has "not been observed" at the unit.
May to July 1973	Bush logs 36 days of duty after he receives special orders to report for duty.
July 30, 1973	Bush's last day in uniform.
Oct. 1, 1973	Bush honorably discharged from the Texas Air National Guard.
May 26, 1974	Bush's scheduled discharge.
Nov. 1974	Bush's final inactive Reserve discharge. He is a full-time student at Harvard Business School.

Chapter 7

Passengers

"I'm not going to cooperate in any way, shape or form. . . .
War is wrong. I don't want any part of it."
--Corbett Bishop, conscientious objector

To a reservist:

3/29/2004

10:53 a.m.

Help

Yes, of course I will help.

Some advice. Apply for a passport right away and get a copy of your birth certificate, educational diplomas and as much documentation as possible, to include your military ID somewhere out of site. Do not carry any military bags or material. It should look like you are a civilian.

Save every penny you can. Have a garage or yard sale. Cash in any savings plans and put everything into cash to include bank accounts. Find a good place to store that cash. Grow your hair and avoid the shaved GI-style haircut. Wear a sports cap to cover up a shaved head. Don't have a drink until you arrive in Canada. A clear mind is important.

You can visit British Columbia, but it should not look like you are moving there.

It should look like you are taking a little vacation. If you have a woman to travel with, so much the better. One of the main tourist destinations in British Columbia is Tofino on the west coast of Vancouver Island. State that you will be visiting for five days.

Remove any military decals from your car.

Your name is not important, nor your present locations. As you probably know, no communication is secure these days.

Be friendly at the border and answer questions but do not be overtalkative. You can have personal items sent to you later or someone else can deliver them to you. Your main objective is to keep your car clear of anything that makes it seem that you are moving to Canada. Keep your suitcases in the trunk out of view and even then don't carry more than what is reasonable for a week's vacation.

Study the area of Tofino online to learn about the whale

migrations tours, Long Beach (a world-class tourist destination) and other interesting places to visit there such as Meares Island.

Cross the border while on leave if you have been called to active duty. Otherwise, if that is not possible, make it during a weekend so that you will be across the border before being missed.

Connect with Brandon's lawyer when you arrive in Canada. I have no legal help in B.C. presently as this is all relatively new.

Whenever you get stressed, remember to take a deep breath and continue to breathe deep; it works like magic. This was very helpful for Brandon when we crossed the border.

Be very specific about when you must be "back at work" from your vacation when asked at the border.

I am explaining as much as possible now, because it might not be possible to reach me if I am picked up, which could happen at any time. I am hardly a secret.

Good luck and feel free to ask about any other details.

Brandon's lawyer, who was a draft resister during the sixties by the way, feels that it could be years before Canada could deport anyone around this issue. Much of law is about delay. By that time, (hopefully) a new administration would be in place that would [be] less of a problem and perhaps offer pardons. That happened during the Carter administration for the draft resisters. Regardless, this decision will change your life forever.

Just one other thought: Consider refusing to comply with orders as an act of civil disobedience. I will forward to you another case where a National Guard sergeant deserted for six months and is now facing a trial in Florida for desertion. It would be an interesting case if you simply refused to cooperate on the grounds of the fact that the USA broke international law [by] invading another sovereign nation. That will be the defense of the sergeant in Florida and it would be useful if a service member in good standing just said "No, I will not cooperate or deploy because my commander in chief has entered this war against Iraq in an illegal and immoral manner." Instead of you being charged, you should receive the Medal of Honor for defending the International Rule of Law and Bush should be tried as a war criminal.

When Thoreau was asked (I believe by Emerson) why he was in jail, he replied why are you not in jail?

I will support your decision whatever you do. If you decide on the decision to refuse to deploy, I would be honored

to handle your case personally and come to wherever you are
in the country to help set up a legal defense (and political
defense) on your behalf.
    Carl Rising-Moore

The border can be difficult to cross. The United States and Canada signed a "Smart Border" declaration on December 12, 2001. According to the declaration, "30 Point Action Plan to Create a Secure and Smart Border," the two countries agree to use biometric identifiers in documentation, review refugee/asylum procedures to ensure applicants are screened for security risks, share information on refugee/asylum claimants, share information on airplane passengers, jointly develop an automated database to share intelligence and "trend analysis," and enable the Royal Canadian Mounted Police to access the FBI fingerprint database via real-time electronic link.

However, it is still possible to cross the border without detection, especially if one uses public transportation.

A long-time Air Force sergeant asked Carl about CO

status or travel to Canada. Would she really need a passport? Where could she find legal representation? Wouldn't her CO application give her commander a warning that she was thinking of deserting? Her First Sergeant had laughed and told her to forget about applying; so many applications were "lost." Carl replied:

3/30/2004

8:45 a.m.

More information.

Hi,

1. The passport is important. It is better to have the bird in hand. Later, you will not be able to apply for the document. It keeps your options open to move to another country than Canada. If necessary, I can do some fund-raising to pay for this and other expenses you may require.

2. Apply for CO status to your commanding officer with a copy and cover letter to your command's legal staff. You have a right to free legal representation from the [military]. Demand it right away. If they put you off, include all this in a bound journal that I recommend you maintain on a daily basis into the future. You never know. The [military] is having problems these days as troops are rotating out of Iraq and telling their friends what a mess the war on Iraq has become.

The CO demand should mention the fact the commander in chief has broken international law in that the USA has invaded a sovereign nation without justification. State that you have now come to a mind-set that believes it is wrong to kill and you want nothing to do with this situation you find yourself [in] that believes it is justifiable to kill others. Find some scripture to support that perspective if you [are] a Christian. Look for a Quaker meetinghouse and obtain some Quaker literature as to killing and war from a philosophical perspective. This demand for CO status should be well written and thought out, as it will be the foundation for all future considerations be it in Canada or the USA or any other country.

Brandon had his deployment moved up one week and was ordered to deploy with only twenty-four hours; notice. Once you register your CO demand, keep your bags packed and be ready to move immediately if you are ordered to sign in to permanent status within a command center.

By contacting Mr. House, you will have initiated a legal status for you in Canada. It is possible for you to live under

CARL RISING-MOORE AND BECKY OBERG

the radar in Canada, howeverit leaves you vulnerable to immediate deportation if discovered by Canadian authorities. It is not necessary for you to be visible to the media, however; if someday you wish to return to the USA, it will be necessary to launch a political as well as legal battle for that return. I understand your desire to remain unknown, and initially that is not a problem, but that may not always be the case in the future to obtain a given result.

You will be charged with desertion, which has no statute of limitations. Eventually, Kerry could offer you a pardon as Carter did during his administration, but that is an unknown. If Bush wins, forget coming back for another four years at least.

Do not believe that you will not be charged if you return. If you returned someday, you would be required to offer your S.S. number for employment and be tracked immediately. Remember, you are considering a life-changing decision. Consider this in all details. You would not be able to tap into that support without becoming a cause celebre. Please consider that you are acting not only for only yourself but for hundreds of thousands of other troops that think in the same manner as you. In the short run, it will not be necessary for you to be visible at all or if everything goes well, perhaps you *can remain unknown for life. You or I have no crystal ball in this regard.*

A work visa may be possible, but only after you have established a status through a lawyer such as Mr. House in establishing some level of status in Canada. Please start your journal right away, because your story would be salable someday and you could support yourself through self-publishing or a sympathetic publisher.

I realize that applying for CO status is going to give your commanding officer a heads-up as to where you are coming from, but it is necessary to do all this with registered mail that is stamped and sealed by a notary public. Map out your plan and be thoughtful about what you are doing. Breathe deep and keep your chin up. You are now in control of your life, no one else.

Carl

The sergeant left for Canada shortly after sending this message. She decided not to go public and adopt an "out of sight, out of mind" approach to dealing with the Canadian government.

Messages continue to come, asking Carl for

help escaping the U.S. A soldier from the Southwest wrote that he had been at Ft. Bragg recently, and had seen pain and confusion in the soldiers who had returned—in his opinion, they were being used as cannon fodder to benefit the elite. He'd been told his college degree would help him advance in the Army, but now people were dying for non-existent weapons to make officers look good. He said he did not want to see our great nation torn apart by an illegal war, and he knew several others who felt the same way.

Uniform Code of Military Justice (UCMJ)
Article 86—Absent Without Leave (AWOL)

Any soldier who, without authority—

a. fails to go to his appointed place of duty at the time prescribed;

b. goes from that place; or

c. absents himself or remains absent from his unit, organization, or place of duty at which he is required to be at the time prescribed; shall be punished as a court-martial may direct.

Another soldier at Ft. Bragg contacted Carl for help. He went AWOL and needed help to move out. He knew the military was searching his home of record, which he was nowhere near. Two others, a man and a woman, were with him—both had served in Iraq and were scheduled to rotate back in. The female even considered getting pregnant to avoid going back.

UCMJ

Article 85—Desertion

Any person found guilty of desertion or attempt to desert shall be punished, if the offense is committed in time of war, by death or such other punishment as a court-martial may direct. . . .

The intent to remain away permanently may be established by circumstantial evidence. Among the circumstances from which an inference may be drawn that an accused intended to remain absent permanently; or that the period of absence was lengthy; that the accused attempted to, or did, dispose of uniforms or other military property; that the accused purchased a ticket for a distant point or was arrested, apprehended, or surrendered a considerable distance from the accused's station; that the accused could have conveniently surrendered to military control but did not; that the accused was dissatisfied with the accused's unit, ship, or with military service; that the accused made remarks indicating an intention to desert; that the accused was under charges or had escaped from confinement at the time of the absence; that the accused made preparations indicative of an intent not to return (for example, financial arrangements); or that the accused enlisted or accepted an appointment in the same or another armed force without disclosing the fact that the accused had not been regularly separated, or entered any foreign armed service without being authorized by the United States. On the other hand, the following are included in the circumstances which may tend to negate an inference that the accused intended to remain away permanently: previous long and excellent service; that the accused left valuable personal property in the unit or on the ship; or that the accused was under the influence of alcohol or drugs during the absence. These lists are illustrative only.

Family members also requested help. One woman wrote:

> *Thank you so much for helping our children. . . . My daughter is in Iraq, her year was up in April and she was extended another 120 days. My son returned from Afghanistan and is at Ft. Bragg currently. He may get sent to Iraq also. My husband is Iraqi and last summer we traveled through Syria and danger into Baghdad. I saw my daughter and we stayed with his family. I was there for three weeks. I was allowed to go on base and see my daughter every day, I also met many Iraqis. I was treated only with kindness by all the Iraqis and Syrians. The guns and RPGs never stopped; you could hear the fights 24/7. I jump now every time a firecracker goes off or a balloon bursts. I won't be able to go to the fireworks this year and I only spent three weeks there. The Iraqis are living in inhuman conditions there that are worse than under Saddam. I will do all I can to help you. I can't donate*

money, but let me know how I can help.

Not everyone deserted. As Carl said, it is best to leave the military by legal means. One Guardsman wrote:

I joined the National Guard to serve in the United States (and of course reap a benefit or two). What did I get? An order to "serve" in Iraq. Should I accept this order and go? Why am I being sent there? Why are Americans in Iraq, killing and dying? These are some questions that I had to ask myself. With only a few days before being activated, I had a lot to think about. There was no answer on earth to these questions that could give me a good enough reason to follow these orders. I was not going to participate in fascist Bush's campaign. And I did not have many options.

So I got in contact with Brandon Hughey via e-mail on my cell phone. He then referred me to Carl Rising-Moore. It seemed unreal talking to these people who were, before this, only names that I had been reading a lot about in Internet news articles. The best plan in my mind at the time was getting to Canada. But I still did not take any action. I knew I had at least a couple months left at the mobilization station before deployment, and I could use this time to plan, or look for other options.

Well here is the punch line: I found another option. Discharge per Chapter 5-13 (personality disorder). This starts by visiting the post-psychology clinic. All that you need to do is be honest about how you feel about being in the military, why you believe you shouldn't be there, how it is affecting you, and how fighting, killing, and death will affect you. If you are willing to take your own life instead of killing others, they will note this as a serious problem. Just be honest about how you feel, and make sure the answers of any written tests you take accurately reflect the feelings you have. You need to let them know that you meet psychiatric criteria for separation in accordance with Chapter 5-13, AR 635-200 and back it up with honest answers. The first psychologist I met with was very helpful, but if you feel that the one you are meeting with is critical of you or things are not working out, get an appointment with another psychologist for a "second opinion." It may even be possible to see a civilian psychologist off post. If possible, this may be the best thing, and even better, if you are a reservist, do this as soon as possible (before you get activated). Oh, one more thing—do not worry about a bad discharge. Unless you have a court-martial, this can only be an honorable discharge.

CARL RISING-MOORE AND BECKY OBERG

This does not always work. It is ultimately the commanding officer's decision on whether or not to discharge a service member. An Air Force member wrote:

I am in the U.S. Air Force based in x, In the next 10 days I am due to be deployed to Iraq for the 2nd time, since I got back from my 1st duty in Iraq I began to suffer with panic attacks, which over time got gradually worse, I recently went into a psychiatric hospital on base, where they stripped me of what little dignity I had left, I had to earn my clothes back and I was just left in a room on my own. The Air Force doctor recommended that I was discharged with an adjustment disorder, to which my commander said no, and I was told that I had signed on the dotted line and I would do my duty for my country. I went and got a second opinion from a civilian psychiatrist, who wrote and told my Air Force doctor I was clinically depressed and that I had a fragile personality due to an abusive upbringing, and to send me to Iraq at this time could make me become actively suicidal. Still I am being told that "I will do my bit for my country." I told my Air Force doctor if they send me down there I will put a gun to my head. I do not believe that we should be there and I want no part of it. I am on tranquilizers and sleeping pills because at this moment in time I am struggling just to cope with daily life. I find Air Force life is a bullying regime and that I am not entitled to an opinion of any sort, all it has done is to try and break me down. Please can you help me before the Air Force destroys my life completely.

And so the Freedom Underground grew.

Chapter 8

Anti-War Soldiers

"War will exist until that distant day when the conscientious objector enjoys the same reputation and prestige that the warrior does today."
—*John F. Kennedy*

I n *Bush at War*, Bob Woodward tells the story of some Special Forces soldiers and CIA paramilitary agents standing over a buried piece of the World Trade Center in Afghanistan. One of them read a prayer, then dedicated the spot to the Americans who died September 11. After vowing America would not let terror win the war, he said, "We will export death and violence to the four corners of the earth in defense of our great nation."

There are some soldiers, however, who refused to be an exporter of death and violence. They preferred to defend our great nation through nonviolent means. These are their stories.

One fine example is Corbett Bishop, a religious objector to military service during World War II. A member of the Church of Christ, he believed war was wrong and refused to cooperate with the authorities, whom he viewed as war makers. He was assigned to a Civilian Public Service camp.

Conscientious objectors either went into a noncombatant role in the military or to a Civilian Public Service camp. Although they had been promised they would do "work of national importance" in the camps, the jobs were often menial. The COs worked nine-hour days, six days a week. They paid the government $35 a month for their room and board. Many left in protest and more than six thousand went to federal prison; in fact, one out of six federal prisoners during World War II was a draft resister.

Bishop was one of the men who left the camp. He was arrested. He said: "The authorities have the power to seize my body; that is all they can do. My spirit will be free." He announced that the authorities would have to seize and imprison his body without any help from him.

He had to be carried into court, and later into prison. He refused to sign any papers, submit to prison procedures, perform assigned work, or make agreements for parole. He went on three hunger strikes, lasting 80, 160 and 250 days. He was force-fed by feeding tube for 144 days. He refused to dress himself and was denied clothes for six months. He even refused to stand up or use a prison toilet. He was pinched until he bruised and he was beaten over the legs with blackjacks. When he was paroled, he refused to cooperate with parole conditions. They threw him in prison again, where the whole ordeal recommenced for 193 days. The authorities, under considerable media pressure, finally released him unconditionally.

Whether one agrees with or despises his stance, it is hard to disagree that Corbett Bishop was truly a free man.

Another good example is Dr. David Wiggins, who went through something similar during the Gulf War. A West Point cadet from 1980 to 1984, he graduated twenty-third in his class and originally wanted to be an infantry general. He writes: "The West Point plan of achieving freedom involved a 'duty concept.' A cadet using the 'duty concept' devoted all the powers of his or her intelligence to twisting logic, distorting facts, rationalizing, and doing whatever was necessary to justify one's orders first to oneself, then to 'the troops.' A cadet was said to have 'internalized' the 'duty concept' when he had completely convinced himself that this was all his own free will. A 'good leader' was someone who excelled at helping others twist logic, distort facts, and rationalize until they, too, believed it was all their own free will. But the West Point method didn't work for me. I kept thinking that intelligence and freedom were the process of reaching decisions based on an objective, independent analysis of the facts, not a foregone conclusion. On the West Point plan, I felt like a tool of the state. I did not feel free."

Why?

"They basically followed orders and I wasn't completely comfortable with that," he said.

He was assigned to the 2nd Battalion of the 158th Air Cavalry regiment at Ft. Hood, Texas. While there, the Cold War ended and the Berlin Wall fell. He was optimistic "for peace and freedom"—until the invasion of Panama, which resulted in the deaths of many civilians. He writes "Apparently, every soldier involved in this assault was able to twist logic, distort facts, rationalize, and do whatever was necessary to justify their orders. I recalled the invasion of the tiny island of Grenada occurring under similar circumstances. I was not aware of a single soldier that had refused either assault. My hopes for success on the 'doctor' plan were dashed. I felt like a maintenance man for the tools of murder and oppression."

He applied for conscientious objector status in February 1990. The Army granted him CO status, but revoked it in August 1990. He writes "I found that the 'CO' plan is a very hard plan to stay on, mainly because of excess commanders. I resigned my commission. My commanders denied it. I attempted to transfer to the Public Health Service—again denied. I offered to repay the entire cost of my education—also denied. I realized that the Army was not concerned with what I thought; it just wanted my body to follow orders. In response, I decided to make my body useless to the Army."

He fasted for twenty-seven days. The Army deployed him to Saudi Arabia, hospitalized him, and threatened to force-feed him under threat of imprisonment. He ate, then began to fast again. The Army shipped him from

Dhahran to King Khalid Military City, which is on the Iraqi border. He writes "Finally, it dawned on me. The Army's purpose is not defending freedom, but imposing control. Freedom is the Army's lady of ill repute. The Army does not love freedom, but they use her allure as bait, and her promises of favors to help them impose control. . . . If I wanted freedom, I would have to take it for myself, hold onto it, and refuse to give it up. . . . The battle lines were drawn. It was the United States Army versus me."

He volunteered for the International Red Cross in Riyadh. He reported his commanders for violations of the Geneva Conventions. He posted notices in the mess hall encouraging soldiers to refuse orders because fighting without a declaration of war was a violation of the Constitution.

"Nobody wanted to go," he said. He objects to war as a way of solving problems.

There is an intersection at King Khalid Military City where two roads converge to form one road. That intersection was always busy with convoys of armored vehicles and supplies heading toward the border. The day after Congress authorized the use of force, he walked into the intersection. As a 2-ton truck approached, Captain Wiggins took off his uniform and stood there in his underwear. He writes: "Traffic backed up quickly. Abrams tanks, Bradley fighting vehicles, various artillery pieces, assorted supply trucks, Hummers, and countless other vehicles sat motionless. I held my outstretched hand against the traffic. My first act as a free man was to do what I could to stop that useless and unnecessary war.

"A crowd of soldiers began to gather beside the road. Some were laughing, some were shouting insults, and some were even shouting encouragement. All these soldiers had other duties they were ignoring while they loitered there entertained by my presence. None of them tried to move me. The 'underpants' method was working! Not only did I feel free, these other soldiers were getting a taste of freedom too!"

Several enlisted personnel watched. "They really didn't know what to do," he said. He was a captain; he outranked them. A sergeant sajor approached and asked him to leave the intersection. He refused. Eventually, a Hummer full of military police pulled up. He sat down and closed his eyes. He was ready to go to jail for his stand. The military police tackled him and threw him in an ambulance. "They thought I was insane," he said.

He was taken to a field hospital. He closed his eyes and refused to talk. A disgusted psychiatrist ruled there was nothing wrong with him.

He was court-martialed after the war ended. Although he was acquitted, he was dismissed. JAG was ordered to reverse the decision, and he was convicted of some minor offenses.

He is now an emergency physician. He writes and speaks against war and counsels conscientious objectors.

Camillo Mejia, a staff sergeant, refused to return to Iraq during the Iraq War. "This is an oil driven war, and I don't think any soldier signs up to fight for oil," the Nicaraguan immigrant said. "I did not sign up for the military to go halfway around the world to be an instrument of oppression. We were all lied to when we were told we were looking for weapons of mass destruction or we were going to fight terrorism. . . . When I saw with my own eyes what war can do to people, a real change began to take place in me. I have witnessed the suffering of a people whose country is in ruins and are further humiliated by the raids, patrols and curfews of an occupying army. My experience of this war has changed me forever. I went to Iraq and was an instrument of violence, and now I have decided to become an instrument of peace." He was charged with desertion. He was convicted and sentenced to a year in prison and a bad-conduct discharge.

As I write this, more than six hundred service members have gone AWOL, according to *The Chicago Tribune*. According to *The New York Times*, the Army granted five conscientious objector discharges in January 2004 alone, compared with thirty-one in 2003, seventeen in 2002, and nine in 2001.

Carl wrote: "To the American, Australian, English, Italian and other soldiers now in Iraq: stop fighting. You can stop this madness now. Today you have the potential to change history, by refusing to kill and by refusing to lose your humanity." He is still waiting for a service member to refuse on conscience to deploy (thus risking jail time) and ask for help in his or her defense.

Sisters and Brothers of the World,

Throughout the course of history, the international community have come together in concert to defeat a common threat.

Today, there is a new threat in Washington, D.C. It is called the Bush Doctrine

On February 15, 2003, you came together in the streets to announce your existence in almost every city on Earth. If your community did not plan a protest of the eminent threat of the Bush Doctrine, you traveled to a sister community to protest the impending illegal war against a sovereign nation.

That day marked the largest political manifestation in the history of our planet.

It was clear from that day on, that although we spoke many different languages from many cultures, we demonstrated for the same values: Peace and Justice.

The Mahatma Gandhi and Dr. Martin Luther King had embodied a different way of fighting, nonviolent direct action, now, we must act again in concert to defeat the most dangerous and destabilizing group of war criminals in history.

Dr. King stated before his assassination that the USA

was the greatest purveyor of violence in the world. That truth is even more evident today in that the USA has troops in the vast majority of countries around the world.

Wherever you live there exists a symbol of United States oppression. The United States is not the only superpower because you, Sisters and Brothers, are the other superpower, but only if we act.

Use your imagination to protest, blockade, climb Big Ben, etc., to make your voice heard in the necessity for regime change in the United States of America.

Do not be afraid of jail. Remember the words of Henry David Thoreau when asked why he was in jail for protesting the invasion of Mexico by the United States of America. He simply asked, "Why are you not here?" If you do go to jail, know that you will not be alone. You will be supported not only by your loving international community, but by history and Thoreau's essay "On Civil Disobedience."

Remember the dual meaning of crisis by the Chinese: danger and opportunity.

If we do not act we are in danger of a group of war criminals succeeding in their grand design to subjugate and control every country on earth. We have the opportunity to remove these criminals from office. These criminals can be located in the capitals of every country that aided and abetted in the illegal overthrow of Iraq. There are those that would ignore the advice of the governed and must be removed from office.

At the same time, those world leaders that protested the war in Iraq must be congratulated for their wisdom and courage to stand up to the Bush/Blair-led war launched by lies and distortion.

Only if we unite at this important moment in world history will we be capable of bringing order and peace. If we hesitate, thinking that someone else will act, then we can only blame ourselves as the fascist few control the silent many.

You have the power to change the world into a kinder and gentler place for future generations. Act. Actions speak louder than words. But your words are also important.

Work politically to remove these criminals from office.

If you can travel to the United States or England, you will find many that will help you fight the Bush/Blair juntas. In 1964, one thousand students from the North of the United States traveled into the Mississippi Delta to join with others from the South to register African Americans to vote. That *dedication was not without cost. Within the first few weeks, four people had been murdered. That was called the "Summer of Freedom." Freedom is not free, again, it is up to you, my Sisters and Brothers. Unite and survive. If we are divided, we will be defeated.*

The people united will never be defeated.

We are the future. We are one. Unite in the Year of Freedom, 2004.

Carl Rising–Moore

Endnotes

Chapter Two notes

"Dear Mark, Just a note": *Manual for Draft-Age Immigrants to Canada*, edited by Mark Satin. House of Anansi, 1968.

Chapter Three notes

"Individuals have international duties": Nuremberg War Crimes Tribunal, quote at www.anti-war.com.

"Preparing for war": Thich Nhat Hanh, quote at www.beliefnet.com.

"How far can you go": Dwight D. Eisenhower, quote at www.anti-war.com.

Chapter Four notes

"We Americans have no commission": President Benjamin Harrison, quote at www.anti-war.com.

"What he was suggesting was a pretext": *Body of Secrets*, by James Bamford. Doubleday, 2001.

"Operation Northwoods called": Bamford, ibid.

"An aircraft at Elgin": Bamford, ibid.

"The Gulf of Tonkin seems right out": Bamford, ibid.

"The existence of the secret government": Bamford, ibid.

Chapter Five notes

"I spent thirty-three years": *War is a Racket!*, by General Smedley Butler. *Common Sense*, 1935.

"When people speak to you": Dwight D. Eisenhower, quote at www.anti-war.com

Chapter Six notes

"The other reality of the spring of 1968": *A Charge to Keep: My Journey to the White House*, by George W. Bush. Perennial, 2001.

"Yale senior George W. Bush rarely": First Son, by Bill Minutaglio. Times Books, 1999.

"Our parents had been in the military": Minutaglio, ibid.

"George and I used to talk": Minutaglio, ibid.

"alternative service": *Shrub: The Short But Happy Political Life of George W. Bush*, by Molly Ivins and Lou Dubose.

"The Army accepted recruits": Ivins, ibid.

"I knew I would serve": Bush.

"I was not prepared to shoot": *First Son*, by Bill Minutaglio. Times Books, 1999.

"There was a five-hundred-man": Minutaglio, ibid.

"I had a lot of requests": Minutaglio, ibid.

"saying so-and-so is interested": "At Height of Vietnam, Bush Picks Guard," by George Lardner, Jr., and Lois Romano. *The Washington Post*, July 28, 1999.

"to return to my unit and fulfill my": *First Son*, by Bill Minutaglio. Times Books, 1999. "Texas National Guard historian Tom Hail said": "Bush's Military Record Reveals Grounding and Absence for Two Full Years," by Robert A. Rogers, Ret. 1st. Lt., mission pilot. Web site: www.logicpathsw.com/AWOLarticle.html.

"was considered a dinosaur and not an integral part of the armed forces": *First Son*, by Bill Minutaglio. Times Books, 1999.

"Several of my fellow pilots had participated": *A Charge to Keep: My Journey to the White House*, by George W. Bush. Perennial, 2001.

"No, I didn't": "Bush Camp's Lies Keep Guard Issue in Spotlight," by Josh Marshall. *The Hill*, February 26, 2004. Web site: www.thehill.com/marshall/022604.aspx.

"I continued flying with my unit": *A Charge to Keep: My Journey to the White House*, by George W. Bush. Perennial, 2001.

"I understand that I may be ordered": Web site: www.users.cis.net/coldfeet.

"Had he reported in": *Is Our Children Learning?*, by Paul Begala. Simon & Schuster, 2000.

"If he did, his drill attendance should": Begala, ibid.

"I remember that I heard": "Bush a No-Show at Alabama Base, Says Memphian," by Jackson Baker. *Memphis Flyer*, 2004.

"I never saw hide nor hair": Baker, ibid.

"virtually impossible": Web site: www.awolbush.com/faq.asp.

"It was just a question of following": *Is Our Children Learning?*, by Paul Begala. Simon & Schuster, 2000.

"There's no excuse for that": "Bush's Loss of Flying Status

Should Have Spurred Probe," by Walter Robinson and Francie Latour. *The Boston Globe*, February 12, 2004.

"Failure to take your flight physical": Robinson, ibid.

"If it didn't happen, that shows": Robinson, ibid.

"good likelihood": "Bush's Partial History," by Bill Morlin and Karen Dorn Steele. *The Spokesman-Review*, March 14, 2004.

"a flagrant dereliction of duty": Morlin, ibid.

"[A] commissioned officer": Web site: www.awolbush.com/deserter.html.

"I also learned the lesson": *A Charge to Keep*, by George W. Bush. HarperCollins, 1999.

Chapter Seven notes

"I'm not going to cooperate": Corbett Bishop, quote at www.blogforamerica.com.

Chapter Eight notes

"War will exist until that distant day": John F. Kennedy, quote at www.duckdaotsu.org.

"We will export death and violence": *Bush at War*, by Bob Woodward. Simon & Schuster, 2002.

"The West Point plan": How to Defeat the United States Army . . . In Your Underpants!, by Dr. David Wiggins. Web site: http://www.duckdaotsu.org.

"Apparently, every soldier involved": Wiggins, ibid.

"I found the CO plan": Wiggins, ibid.

"Finally, it dawned on me": Wiggins, ibid.

"Traffic backed up quickly": Wiggins, ibid.

"This is an oil-driven war": Staff sergeant Camilo Meija, quote at www.notinourname.net.

Bibliography

Books

Body of Secrets, by James Bamford. Doubleday, 2001.

Bush at War, by Bob Woodward. Simon and Schuster, 2002.

A Charge to Keep: My Journey to the White House, by George W. Bush. Perennial, 2001.

First Son: George W. Bush and the Bush Family Dynasty, by Bill Minutaglio. Times Books, 1999.

Is Our Children Learning? The Case Against Prezident George W. Bush, by Paul Begala. Simon & Schuster, 2000.

On Civil Disobedience, by Henry David Thoreau.

A Pretext for War: 9/11, Iraq, and the Abuse of America's Intelligence Agencies, by James Bamford. Doubleday, 2004.

Shrub: The Short but Happy Political Life of George W. Bush, by Molly Ivins and Lou Dubose. Vintage Books, 2002.

Tao-te Ching (a new English version), by Stephen Mitchell. Perennial Classics, 2000.

Articles

"At Height of Vietnam, Bush Picks Guard," by George Lardner Jr. and Lois Romano. *The Washington Post*, July 28, 1999.

"Bush a No-Show at Alabama Base, Says Memphian," by Jackson Baker. Web site: www.memphisflyer.com/content.asp?ID=2834&onthefly=1.

"Bush camp's lies keep Guard issue in spotlight," by Josh Marshall. *The Hill*, February 26, 2004. Web site: www.thehill.com/marshall/022604.aspx.

"Bush's Loss of Flying Status Should Have Spurred Probe," by Walter V. Robinson and Francie Latour. *The Boston Globe*, February 12, 2004.

"Bush's Military Record Reveals Grounding and Absence for Two Full Years," by Robert A. Rogers, Ret. 1st Lt., mission pilot. Web site: www.logicpathsw.com/AWOLarticle.html.

Web Sites

Bush's military records. Web site: www.users.cis.net/coldfeet/document.htm. See also www.awolbush.com.

Project for the New American Century. Web site: www.newamericancentury.org. (Note: This site is down frequently, but is still highly recommended by the authors.)

Resources for Conscientious Objectors

Note: Not all of these organizations counsel desertion. They are listed strictly because they offer advice and assistance to service members who can no longer fight for reasons of conscience.

American Friends Service Committee.

Central Committee for Conscientious Objectors. 405 14th Street #205, Oakland, CA 94612. http://www.objector.org

G.I. Rights Hotline. 1-800-394-9544.

Jeffry A. House, Barrister and Solicitor. 31 Prince Arthur Avenue. Toronto, Ontario M5R 1B2 Canada. Tel. 416-926-9402. Fax 416-960-5456.

Military Families Speak Out (MFSO). P.O. Box 549, Jamaica Plain, MA 02130. 617-522-9323. http://www.mfso.org mfso@mfso.org

National Lawyers Guild. http://www.nlg.org

Quaker House. Chuck Fager, director. 910-923-3912. http://www.quakerhouse.org chuckfager@aol.com

Contributions for current and future Freedom Underground passengers may be made at: Dove Legal Defense Fund, Attorney Jeffry House, 31 Prince Arthur Ave., Toronto, Ontario M5R 1B2, Canada. "Dove Legal Defense Fund" or something similar should be written in the check's memo section.